W9-BZS-114

Al Gore

The People to Know Series

Neil Armstrong
*The First Man
on the Moon*
0-89490-828-6

Isaac Asimov
*Master of
Science Fiction*
0-7660-1031-7

Robert Ballard
*Oceanographer Who
Discovered the* Titanic
0-7660-1147-X

Willa Cather
Writer of the Prairie
0-89490-980-0

Bill Clinton
*United States
President*
0-89490-437-X

Hillary Rodham Clinton
Activist First Lady
0-89490-583-X

Bill Cosby
Actor and Comedian
0-89490-548-1

Walt Disney
*Creator of
Mickey Mouse*
0-89490-694-1

Bob Dole
Legendary Senator
0-89490-825-1

Marian Wright Edelman
*Fighting for
Children's Rights*
0-89490-623-2

Bill Gates
*Billionaire
Computer Genius*
0-89490-824-3

Jane Goodall
Protector of Chimpanzees
0-89490-827-8

Al Gore
*Leader for the
New Millennium*
0-7660-1232-8

Tipper Gore
*Activist, Author,
Photographer*
0-7660-1142-9

Ernest Hemingway
Writer and Adventurer
0-89490-979-7

Ron Howard
*Child Star &
Hollywood Director*
0-89490-981-9

John F. Kennedy
*President of the
New Frontier*
0-89490-693-3

John Lennon
The Beatles and Beyond
0-89490-702-6

Maya Lin
Architect and Artist
0-89490-499-X

Jack London
*A Writer's
Adventurous Life*
0-7660-1144-5

Barbara McClintock
*Nobel Prize
Geneticist*
0-89490-983-5

Christopher Reeve
*Hollywood's Man
of Courage*
0-7660-1149-6

Ann Richards
*Politician, Feminist,
Survivor*
0-89490-497-3

Sally Ride
*First American Woman
in Space*
0-89490-829-4

Will Rogers
*Cowboy
Philosopher*
0-89490-695-X

Franklin D. Roosevelt
*The Four-Term
President*
0-89490-696-8

Steven Spielberg
*Hollywood
Filmmaker*
0-89490-697-6

Martha Stewart
*Successful
Businesswoman*
0-89490-984-3

Amy Tan
Author of
The Joy Luck Club
0-89490-699-2

Alice Walker
Author of
The Color Purple
0-89490-620-8

Simon Wiesenthal
*Tracking Down
Nazi Criminals*
0-89490-830-8

Frank Lloyd Wright
*Visionary
Architect*
0-7660-1032-5

People to Know

Al Gore

Leader for the
New Millennium

Laura S. Jeffrey

Enslow Publishers, Inc.

40 Industrial Road   PO Box 38
Box 398   Aldershot
Berkeley Heights, NJ 07922   Hants GU12 6BP
USA   UK

http://www.enslow.com

Library of Congress Cataloging-in-Publication Data

Jeffrey, Laura S.
    Al Gore : leader for the new millennium / Laura S. Jeffrey.
        p. cm. — (People to know)
    Includes bibliographical references (p.) and index.
    Summary: Surveys the childhood, military career, and political activities of the
man who served as vice president under Bill Clinton.
    ISBN 0-7660-1232-8
    1. Gore, Albert, 1948– —Juvenile literature. 2. Vice-Presidents—United States—
Biography—Juvenile literature. [1. Gore, Albert, 1948– . 2. Vice-Presidents.]
I. Title. II. Series.
E840.8.G65J44 1999
973.929′092
[b]—DC21   98-52498
                                                    CIP
                                                        AC

Printed in the United States of America

10 9 8 7 6 5 4 3 2 1

To Our Readers:
All Internet addresses in this book were active and appropriate when we went to press.
Any comments or suggestions can be sent by e-mail to Comments@enslow.com or to
the address on the back cover.

Illustration Credits:
AP/Wide World Photos, pp. 26, 51, 64; *Carthage Courier*, p. 38; © Corel
Corporation, p. 96; Library of Congress, pp. 29, 33, 58, 73, 78, 89; Office of
the Vice President, pp. 13, 16, 71; Office of the Vice President, photo by
Thomas Shelby, p. 93; Official White House Photo, p. 9, 45, 62; St. Albans
School, pp. 18, 20.

Cover Illustration: Official White House Photo

Contents

A Fateful Phone Call

Years later, Tipper Gore remembered the telephone call that changed her husband's life forever. It was late when the phone rang, and it was hot—a typical summer evening on the beloved family farm in Carthage, Tennessee. United States Senator Al Gore, Jr., his wife, and three of their four children had left their stately old Tudor home in Arlington, Virginia, for some rest and relaxation at their farm. It was just a hop, skip, and a jump from the farm where Al had spent his summers growing up. As usual, Al Gore's schedule during the past several months had been hectic. Aside from his Senate duties, he had been traveling regularly to Tennessee to meet with his constituents— the people he represented. He also was writing a book on the environment, a subject about which Gore is passionate.

Gore had also been keeping a close eye on the presidential campaign. After some dramatic moments, Arkansas governor Bill Clinton had won the necessary delegate votes in state primaries to become the Democratic nominee for president. In a few weeks, Clinton would officially be nominated at the Democratic National Convention in New York.

As for Gore? Been there, done that. He ran for president once but dropped out of the primaries after failing to get enough support. But it was not with jealousy or envy that Gore was keeping track of this year's proceedings. He had made a thoughtful decision not to run, even though some people believed he was the best hope the Democrats had to unseat President George Bush.

Gore had decided not to run because not too long before, his personal life had been in turmoil. A terrible accident had almost taken the life of his youngest child and only son, Albert III. Gore had taken a long, hard look at himself in the weeks and months after the accident. He changed his priorities: Family would come first. Young Albert's recuperation had been long and difficult, but the boy was finally healed. Emotionally, the entire family felt better. Gore was now ready to plunge back into politics—but not to run for president.

Gore did not know Bill Clinton well. They had talked at length once in 1988, and again only a few weeks before the night of the fateful phone call. Their second meeting had lasted several hours. Clinton

Al Gore, Jr.

had asked Gore if he would consider being Clinton's running mate. Gore said yes. But he did not want to be a traditional vice president. He wanted to be a partner in leadership. Gore had laid out a lot of conditions for accepting the vice presidency. Clinton had been friendly, but he had not offered Gore the job. He was talking to other candidates as well.

The news media had learned that Gore was on the "short list" of vice presidential prospects. With the convention a few weeks away, it was time for Clinton to make a decision. If Clinton chose Gore, the media wanted to be there to capture the moment. Reporters and photographers parked at the edge of the Gores' property and waited.

At 11:00 P.M. on July 7, 1992, the telephone rang at the Carthage farm. Gore's wife, Tipper, answered the phone. "Hi, Tipper," presidential candidate Bill Clinton responded. "I hope I didn't wake you up; and if I did, I needed to."[1] Clinton asked to speak to Al. Tipper put down the phone and called for him. Gore usually turned in early, but this night he was still awake. It was then that Clinton asked Gore to be his running mate.

"[I was] pleased, supportive, and excited," Tipper recalled later. She thought her husband's presence on the ticket would make it "a winning combination."[2]

Why did Clinton choose Gore? "The big factor was the personal and political comfort level Bill felt with Gore," said a senior Clinton adviser. "Every time, Bill would come away from a conversation with Gore and say, 'He's so smart.'"[3]

Smart. Funny. A strong sense of loyalty to family

and country. These qualities made Gore an appealing political partner for Clinton. Gore had many other qualities that led Clinton to him. Clinton was a newcomer to the national political scene. Gore, on the other hand, was very familiar with the ways of Washington. In fact, this son of a prominent congressman seemed almost destined for higher office.

2

Big Al, Little Al

From the time he was a young boy, Al Gore was surrounded by politics. Albert Arnold Gore, Jr., was born on March 31, 1948, in Washington, D.C. He was the second child of Albert Gore, Sr., and his wife, Pauline. The Gores also had a daughter, Nancy. She was ten years old when her baby brother was born.

Al Sr. was from a small farm town in Tennessee. He had been a teacher and a lawyer before becoming interested in politics. In 1938, he was elected to represent Tennessee as a Democrat in the United States House of Representatives. Two years later, he made headlines by volunteering to serve in the military during World War II. Congressmen were exempt from military service, and he was the first to waive the

With his big sister, Nancy, at the wheel of their jeep, Al Jr. enjoyed riding with his family around their 250-acre farm in Tennessee.

exemption. He joined the Army as a private, the lowest rank. He served honorably, and then returned to Congress. He had been a congressman for eight years when Al Jr. was born.

Pauline was also from a small farm community in Tennessee. She was a woman ahead of her time. She met Al Sr. when they were both law students. Pauline was one of the first two women to earn a law degree from Vanderbilt University. She became a lawyer in an era when few women graduated from college. After marrying, Pauline quit her job. She devoted her time not only to her children but also to her husband's career. She was very active in his political campaigns. She even volunteered at his congressional office.

By 1952, Al Gore, Sr., had served in the House of Representatives for twelve years. He decided to challenge Kenneth D. McKellar in the Democratic primary for his Senate seat. McKellar had represented Tennessee in the Senate for thirty-five years. He was a very popular and powerful figure. Many believed Al Sr. did not stand a chance of winning. The Gores ran an enthusiastic campaign. Little Al, as his son was called, was four years old.

Pauline Gore told a reporter for the *Saturday Evening Post* that year that despite his age, Little Al wanted to help his father get elected. "One afternoon I took Little Al and a girl playmate in the car after some ice cream," she recalled. "A policeman was riding ahead of us, and Little Al said, 'If we can catch up with him, I'll ask him to vote for my daddy.'"[1]

"Well, we didn't catch up," Pauline continued, "so

the little girl said, 'Maybe he'll vote for your daddy anyhow.' 'No,' said Little Al. 'You've got to ask 'em!'"[2]

Al Sr. defeated McKellar and became a senator in 1952. His power and influence grew. The Democratic Party considered nominating him for vice president in 1956. Republican President Dwight D. Eisenhower and his running mate, Vice President Richard M. Nixon, went on to win the election.

"Growing up, I watched [my father] stand courageously for civil rights, economic opportunity and a government that worked for ordinary people," Al Jr. said in a speech years later.[3] He also said that his father and mother never pressured him to pursue a political career. "When I was growing up, I don't ever remember a time when either of my parents said: 'Don't you want to go into politics? Don't you think you would like do this or that?' I don't ever remember a time."[4] Said Al's mother, Pauline Gore, "We brought him up to do a good job in whatever he chose to do."[5]

During his youth, Little Al experienced a kind of double life. Part of the year, he and his family lived in an exclusive hotel in Washington. He attended a prestigious private school, St. Albans School for Boys. His family socialized with noted politicians of the day, including Nixon and John F. Kennedy. In fact, Albert Gore, Sr., worked on the campaign to elect Kennedy president in 1960.

Al Jr. spent his summers on his family's farm in Carthage, a small town about sixty miles east of Nashville. There, he lived as a country boy. He milked cows, rode horses, and canoed on the river. He later said that while he appreciated his lifestyle in

Senator Al Gore, Sr., was an excellent fiddler, much to the delight of his young son.

Washington, he most enjoyed his time on the farm in Tennessee. "It was in Tennessee that I developed an appreciation for strong family ties and hard physical labor—getting up long before the sun, working a couple of hours until breakfast, working till lunch, then after dinner helping a neighbor take up hay," Gore said.[6]

Whether he was in the city or the country, Al impressed people. He was popular, physically active, and intelligent. At St. Albans, Al was class treasurer for two years. He was a member of the Government Club and Glee Club, among other activities. He also played football and basketball and ran track. During his senior year, Al was named captain of the football team.

His activities did not overshadow his academic achievements, however. He earned top grades and won a National Merit scholarship. Al also developed a close relationship with his sister, Nancy, despite their ten-year age difference. Nancy gave Al support, advice, and encouragement in all his efforts.

In May 1965, shortly before he graduated from high school, Al attended his senior prom with a date. There he met a pretty blond girl who was someone else's date. Her name was Mary Elizabeth Aitcheson, but everybody called her "Tipper." This was a nickname her mother had given her when she was a baby. Tipper was a junior at St. Agnes Episcopal School for Girls in Alexandria, Virginia. Tipper's parents had divorced when she was two years old. She lived in her grandmother's house in Arlington with her grandmother and mother. As an only child, she later recalled

Al Gore was a top student at St. Albans School for Boys, an exclusive private school in Washington, D.C.

her childhood as lonely. Tipper saw her father weekly, but divorce was uncommon when she was growing up, and she was sometimes teased about it at school.

Al's brief encounter with Tipper at the prom obviously left a lasting impression. The next day, he called and asked her out on a date. Tipper accepted. They soon became a couple. "He was sexy, serious, smart, and funny," Tipper recalled. "Funny is real important to me."[7] Later that summer, Al invited Tipper to visit his family on their beloved farm in Carthage. The Gores liked Tipper, and she returned their warm feelings. They were "very easy to get along with, very down to earth," she said.[8] It was not long before Al and Tipper began dating exclusively.

Al graduated from high school in 1965. That fall, he enrolled at Harvard University in Cambridge, Massachusetts. At the time, American society was in turmoil because the United States had become deeply involved in the Vietnam War. Many Americans did not support the war. First, the United States Congress had not officially declared war, which is required by the Constitution. Also, the war's objectives were unclear. As a result, few young men volunteered to serve in the military. The United States government began drafting young men—requiring them to join the military and become involved in the war effort. As the war progressed, thousands of young American men were injured or killed in combat. Opposition grew even stronger.

College students, in particular, were vocal in their opposition to the war. They organized protests and marches and burned their draft cards. Some even fled

Gore's high school yearbook picture in 1965. "It won't be long before he reaches the top," predicted the yearbook editor.

to Canada and other countries that provided shelter to the so-called draft dodgers.

Al Gore, Jr., was against the war. He once wrote a letter to his father, explaining his views. That letter would surface years later in an attempt to harm Gore Jr.'s political career. Despite his strong feelings, Gore Jr. did not become too involved in the antiwar movement. Instead, he continued his record of achievement. He was elected class president his freshman year. Throughout college, he studied hard and made good grades. He developed a reputation as hardworking, serious, and methodical.

Gore also remained close to his parents. In 1968, he helped his father write a speech in support of Eugene McCarthy's campaign for the Democratic presidential nomination. One of McCarthy's challengers was Hubert Humphrey, who had been vice president under President Lyndon Johnson. As John F. Kennedy's vice president, Johnson became president when Kennedy was assassinated in 1963. Johnson was elected president for a full term in 1964. He increased American involvement in Vietnam, which angered voters as well as fellow Democratic Party leaders. Johnson decided not to run for reelection in 1968.

McCarthy was billed as the "peace candidate," while Humphrey was negatively associated with Johnson's Vietnam policies. Still, Humphrey became the party's nominee. He lost the election to Republican Richard Nixon.

During his college years, Al made many close friends. One of his roommates and best friends was Tommy Lee Jones, a Harvard football player. Jones went on to become an actor. In 1994, he won an Academy Award for Best Supporting Actor for his role in *The Fugitive*. Gore also became friends with Erich Segal, who then taught at Harvard. In 1970, Segal wrote *Love Story*, a novel that was turned into a popular movie starring Ryan O'Neal and Ali McGraw. O'Neal played Oliver Barrett III, a character who felt pressure from his father to follow in the family footsteps. Segal later said that he based the Barrett character partly on Al Gore, Jr.

Tipper graduated from high school in 1966. She went to a junior college in Boston so that she and Al could continue to see each other. "We felt very strongly about each other and we wanted to be close," she said.[9] After two years, Tipper transferred to Boston University and studied child psychology. She and Al continued their relationship. Finally, during his senior year in college, Gore proposed marriage. "We had gone out to dinner and we were walking by the Charles River," Tipper recalled years later. "He had this beautiful ring. It was a very romantic proposal."[10] They made plans to get married after Tipper finished college.

Al Gore graduated from Harvard in May 1969 with a bachelor's degree in government. His senior thesis was titled "The Impact of Television on the Conduct of the Presidency, 1947–1969." Immediately after graduation, Gore faced one of the first big dilemmas of his life. As a college student, he had been exempt from the military draft. Now, however, he would likely be drafted. What should he do? He certainly did not want to fight in a war he did not believe in. As the son of an influential senator, he could have pulled strings to avoid being drafted.

Yet Al Gore knew that his decision affected others besides him. "In Carthage, Tennessee, it was no secret who was on the draft board, what the rough quota was each month," Gore recalled years later. "And if you didn't go, it was no secret that one of your friends would have to go in your place."[11]

There was also Al Sr. to consider. At the time, the elder Gore was a member of the Senate Foreign Relations Committee. Through his work on the committee, he came to believe that President Nixon and his aides were purposely misleading Americans about the extent of United States involvement in the war. Senator Gore became an outspoken opponent of the war and rallied other congressman to his cause. This greatly angered President Nixon. "[My father] was a real hero—he had guts," Al Jr. said later.[12]

The elder Gore's views on Vietnam hurt him politically. When it came time for reelection, he faced a heated battle from Republican challenger William Brock. Al Jr. did not want his decision on the draft to become an issue in his father's reelection campaign.

Senator Gore and his wife told their son that they would support whatever decision he made. "If you want to go to Canada" to avoid the draft, his mother told him, "I'll go with you."[13] But in the end, Al Jr. decided to face his future without special favors. Perhaps he was acting on advice his parents once gave him: "Tell the truth and always love [your] country."[14] He enlisted in the Army in the summer of 1969, leaving Tipper behind to finish her final year of college.

3

Reporting for Duty

Al Gore, Jr., enlisted in the Army in 1969. First, he was sent to basic training at Fort Dix in New Jersey. Then he reported for duty at Fort Rucker in Alabama. That Army post was the training ground for helicopter crews. Young men came to the post to learn how to fly helicopters and then were sent to Vietnam for combat.

Gore was an information specialist. He wrote press releases and articles for the post newspaper. When he was younger, Gore had met journalist friends of his sister, Nancy. He had been interested in learning more about journalism. Now he had that opportunity. Yet Gore knew that because of the troop buildup overseas, it was only a matter of time before he received orders sending him to Vietnam.

Meanwhile, Mary Elizabeth "Tipper" Aitcheson continued studying child psychology at Boston University in Massachusetts. She completed her degree in May 1970. Gore took a leave from the Army, and he and Tipper got married. They wed on May 19, 1970, at National Cathedral in Washington, D.C. Gore wore his formal Army uniform. Tommy Lee Jones, Gore's former roommate and an up-and-coming actor, was one of the groomsmen. Al's sister, Nancy, was Tipper's matron of honor.

After their honeymoon, the newlyweds moved to a trailer park in Daleville, Alabama, a few miles from the Army post. Gore continued his work at Fort Rucker and proved to be an excellent soldier. He was selected Soldier of the Month in May 1970 and was given a $50 savings bond. A few months later, in November 1970, Albert Gore, Sr., narrowly lost his Senate seat to William Brock. It had been a bitter campaign, with Brock accusing Gore Sr. of being soft on communism. Some people believed Brock had received campaign help from Nixon administration officials because Gore's antiwar views had angered Nixon.

Senator Gore had enjoyed a long and distinguished political career. Among his other achievements, he sponsored the Interstate Highway Act. This act standardized highway signs and markings across the United States. He also worked to resolve the energy crisis of the 1970s and had supported legislation that furthered civil rights. "When I was in the Senate, I always thought it my duty to represent the people who least knew of their need for representation," he

Pauline and Senator Al Gore, Sr., congratulate newlyweds Tipper and Al Jr.

said later. "The young, the poor, the disadvantaged, these were the people I thought most of."[1]

Senator Gore made a smooth transition to private life. He was named to the board of directors of several corporations. He and Pauline opened a law firm. Still, Al Gore, Jr., was discouraged by what had happened to his father. At that moment, a political career was far from his mind. "Al looked upon his father as a great, dedicated, caring, sensitive, patriotic servant," said a longtime Gore family friend. "And Al Gore felt that his father, on the basis of all that and on the basis of his intelligence . . . simply deserved to be elected."[2]

By the end of 1970, Gore had received orders to go to Vietnam. He left Tipper in Alabama, and in January 1971 he reported for duty at a military base near Saigon. Military buddies later remembered Gore as a regular guy who not only performed his duties but also borrowed cigarettes and gave hilarious impressions of superior officers who annoyed him.[3] Overseas, Gore had long discussions with fellow soldiers about the war. "We felt the military was an obligation," one later said, "even though we disagreed with what was going on."[4]

As an information specialist, Gore was never in actual combat. However, he saw and heard about things that bothered him. He wrote letters to friends, telling them that if he survived, he would go to divinity school to atone for his sins.[5]

Occasionally, Gore sent his wife copies of the articles he wrote for military newspapers. Tipper sent them to John Seigenthaler. He was editor of *The Tennessean*, a newspaper based in Nashville. Seigenthaler, who was active in the Democratic Party, knew Al Gore, Sr. In fact, the elder Gore had already shared with Seigenthaler a letter that Gore Jr. had sent to his father from Vietnam. Seigenthaler told the elder Gore he was impressed with his son's writing ability.

Gore's tour of duty in Vietnam ended in June 1971, and he resigned from the Army. He returned to the United States a man changed by his experiences. He later said that while he still believed the war was wrong, he understood why some people thought it was important to intervene. He called his military service one of the most important growth experiences of his life.

Gore learned that John Seigenthaler had been impressed with his writing. Gore called the editor, who invited Gore to interview for a job. Gore met with Frank Ritter, the city editor. Ritter always asked job applicants the same question: What would you do if an editor ordered you to write a story that you knew to be untrue?

"I can't imagine that an editor would ever ask a reporter to do that," Gore replied. "It would be unprofessional. But if it happened, I would resign before I violated my conscience." Ritter called Gore's response "the best answer I've ever gotten."[6]

In 1971, Al and Tipper Gore moved to Nashville and rented a house. Gore began working on the night shift as a reporter for *The Tennessean*. Gore's parents invited him to attend political functions, but he said no. He had no interest in politics. He told his editors he did not want to even write about politics.

Gore started his career at *The Tennessean* writing about parades and festivals. Soon, he progressed to more serious topics. Like other reporters of his day, Gore hammered out stories on an electric typewriter. He often penciled in many changes before turning over the pages to an editorial staff.

During the day, Gore attended graduate divinity courses at Vanderbilt University. "Because of the soul-searching I had gone through over the decision to serve, I wanted a structured opportunity to explore the deeper questions in my life," Gore explained.[7]

Many Americans protested against the Vietnam War. Gore, too, believed the war was wrong, but he said his military service in Vietnam was one of the most important growth experiences of his life.

Said Tipper, "I think it was a purification."[8] Professors later described Gore as motivated and intelligent.

Tipper, meanwhile, enrolled in a photography course. She became a skilled photographer and eventually got a part-time job at *The Tennessean*. She also began graduate work in psychology. Later, she earned a master's degree in the subject.

On the job, Gore's feelings about politics changed. He began writing stories about local politicians and how city government worked. Gore developed a reputation for being curious, aggressive, and tenacious. These were qualities all good reporters have. His editors believed that he was talented and would make journalism his lifelong career.

Tipper Gore later described her husband as restless and unsure of what he wanted to do with his life. Yet she also said she never lost confidence that he would be successful at whatever he chose. Aside from divinity school and journalism, Gore became involved in a home-building and land-development company. Later, he was a farmer of sorts, raising livestock and growing tobacco. He and Tipper bought a farm in Carthage, across the river from Gore's childhood farm. They also purchased a house in Nashville.

In August 1973, the Gores' first daughter, Karenna, was born. Also that year, Gore began an exciting assignment for *The Tennessean*. A local developer told Gore that a member of the city council had approached him for a bribe. On the advice of the paper's editors, Gore contacted state law officials. Together, they worked out a sting operation. The developer, wearing a hidden microphone, arranged to meet the councilman to talk about the bribe. Gore and some police officers waited in their cars, listening to and recording the conversation through equipment they had installed in their vehicles. Gore and the others could clearly hear the councilman tell the developer that he would get a zoning ordinance passed if the developer gave him some money.

The councilman was charged with seeking a bribe, and a trial was scheduled. Gore wrote about the incident for *The Tennessean*. However, a judge ruled that the tapes could not be used as evidence, and a jury acquitted the councilman. He continued his political career.

Gore later said he was shocked that the law had enabled the councilman to go free. It spurred him to want to learn more about the legal system. Gore left divinity school and began taking classes at Vanderbilt Law School, where his mother had earned her law degree.

Gore took a leave of absence from the newspaper, but he returned in 1974 as an editorial writer. Meanwhile, he continued law classes. An interest in politics was sparked. Gore began to believe that politics would be a way for him to change the things he did not like about the world. The one aspect he most enjoyed about reporting was gathering information. As a politician, he could still gather information. Then he could use his knowledge to bring about change.

In February 1976, Seigenthaler learned that long-time Tennessee congressman Joe Evins was retiring from the United States Congress. Evins held the Fourth Congressional District seat. It was the same seat that Al Gore, Sr., had held more than thirty years previously, before he began his Senate career. The district included Carthage, where Al Gore, Jr., now had a farm.

On impulse, Seigenthaler called his young reporter to tell him the news. Later, Gore said that he had not been talking about entering politics. But as soon as he heard of the opportunity, his mind was made up. He hung up the telephone and told Tipper he was going to run for Congress. Then he dropped to the floor and did a few push-ups, as a symbolic way of getting prepared. "It just came home to me that if I was ever going to do it [run for office], now was the time," he later explained. "Not ten years from now. Not one week from now. Now."[9]

"He really does believe that he was born to lead," said Leon Wieseltier, a friend of Gore's who is also a journalist. "He believes he is a historical figure. And in American politics a sense of destiny doesn't hurt."[10] Said Gore's mother, Pauline, "He could lead, and if he could, he *should.*"[11]

That night, Gore called his father and told him he was going to run for office. "Well, son, I'll vote for you," his father replied, surprised but happy.[12] Later, Gore Sr. said that he was ready "to give my hillbilly speeches to elect my boy to Congress. But Gore Jr. said, 'Hold on, Dad. I want to win this one myself.'"[13] Al Gore, Sr., followed his son's wishes. He did not make any speeches during his son's first campaign.

A few days after Gore made his decision, family members and friends gathered at the county courthouse in Carthage. Gore was nervous; he had thrown up before leaving the house. But he was ready to make his first political speech. He announced his candidacy for the United States House of Representatives.

Gore had been around politics and politicians for most of his life. At one time, he was unsure of what he wanted to do. At another point in his life, he was disillusioned and had no interest in following in his father's footsteps. Now, however, the twenty-seven-year-old was ready. Gore wanted a career in public service so that he could change people's lives for the better.

In 1976, Al Gore decided to run for Congress.

On the Political Scene

Albert Gore, Jr., announced his candidacy for the United States House of Representatives in the winter of 1976. The field was crowded: Seven other candidates ran against him in the Democratic primary. The Gore name, however, was familiar to the voters in Tennessee's Fourth District. He also had his own, compelling message. He vowed to raise taxes for wealthy people, create more job opportunities, and cut defense spending.

Gore's top challenger for the nomination, Stanley Rogers, tried to paint Gore as a rich man disconnected from ordinary people. In the end, the voters were not persuaded by Rogers' message. Gore won the primary by a narrow margin.

Facing an independent candidate in the November

general election, Gore won handily. He was now United States Representative Al Gore, Democrat from Tennessee. Shortly after his victory, he, Tipper, and toddler Karenna moved to the Washington, D.C., area. They settled in the brick, Tudor-style house in Arlington, Virginia, where Tipper grew up.

The next several years were busy ones for the Gores, professionally as well as personally. Their daughter Kristin was born in June 1977. In 1978, Gore ran unopposed for a second term in office. In January 1979, daughter Sarah was born. Two months later, Gore became the first House member to be televised during regular congressional proceedings. In 1980, Gore was elected to a third term. He received 79 percent of the vote. That year, he helped pass the Superfund law to clean up hazardous chemical dump sites.

In 1982, the state of Tennessee was redistricted, and Gore was switched to Tennessee's Sixth District. But that did not deter him. He ran unopposed and was reelected to a fourth term in office. A month before, in October 1982, the Gore's fourth child, Albert III, was born. "We wanted a large family because I was an only child and felt short-changed," Tipper Gore once said.[1]

As a congressman, Gore used his reporter's skills to thoroughly investigate a wide range of issues. He was perhaps most interested in environmental causes. In fact, he first became worried about global warming back in the 1960s, long before it became a popular issue. Gore organized the first congressional hearings on toxic waste.

Gore traveled frequently to his farm in Tennessee. In his home state, he met with the men and women who had elected him to office. Political analysts praised the privileged, well-educated man's ability to connect not only with the wealthy but also with his middle-class and poor constituents.

Gore held regular meetings where he invited voters to discuss issues with him. During his congressional career, he met with his constituents almost two thousand times. "Instead of telling people what to do," Gore said, "we should listen and learn how to give them the tools to do what they want."[2]

One magazine reported an incident that was typical of Gore. During a speech to students in Tennessee, he discovered a majority of them feared that a nuclear war would occur in their lifetime. He vowed to learn more about the subject. Gore returned to Washington and set up a study schedule. During the next year, he spent eight hours every week researching the issues and consulting with experts. He himself became known as an expert on nuclear issues.

Gore also found time for relaxation. He played basketball in the House gym with other congressmen. Late at night, when he was alone, Gore lay on the gym floor and hurled the ball at the hoop. When he had perfected the shot, he unveiled it to his teammates and opponents.[3]

Like his father, Gore soon found an opportunity to run for the Senate. In January 1983, Senator Howard Baker announced he would not seek reelection. Baker was the senior Republican senator from Tennessee. Gore immediately announced his Senate candidacy.

In the 1984 election, he claimed an easy victory over two opponents.

Gore was interviewed by *U.S. News and World Report* shortly after the election. The freshman senator said he intended to focus on environmental issues. He wanted to see the government continue cleaning up toxic-waste sites, reauthorize the Clean Air Act, and fund wastewater-treatment projects.[4]

As he did earlier in his career, Gore impressed people with his intensity and attention to detail. He was part of the Senate committee that investigated the 1986 explosion of the space shuttle *Challenger*. His research revealed that the National Aeronautics and Space Administration had reduced its quality-control staff in the years leading up to the disaster.

Gore also pushed for sterner warnings on tobacco products. This surprised some people, since Gore represented a state with thousands of tobacco farmers. Gore himself had grown tobacco on his Tennessee farm. Yet Gore believed warning labels on tobacco products were justified. "There is great value in sticking to your guns when you feel you're right about a subject," Gore once said, "even if that means certain defeat."[5] Gore added that he had learned this lesson from his father.

Gore's stand on tobacco certainly was affected by the death of his beloved sister. Nancy Gore was an achiever in her own right. She had helped found the Peace Corps in the 1960s, for example. But more important to Al, she had been his closest adviser and confidante. Her death from lung cancer during her brother's first Senate campaign had devastated

When he was elected to the Senate in 1984, Gore said he would focus on environmental issues.

Gore. "She was a terribly important part of Al's life," Tipper Gore said. "She was a mediator, adviser, powerful supporter and loving critic."[6]

During a speech years later, Gore said his sister began smoking when she was thirteen years old. At the time, the health risks were not known. By the time she knew smoking was dangerous, she was addicted and could not quit. Gore held her hand while she died a painful death.

"Tomorrow morning another thirteen-year-old girl will start smoking." Gore said in the speech. "Three thousand young people in America will start smoking tomorrow. One thousand of them will die a death not unlike my sister. And that is why, until I draw my last breath, I will pour my heart and my soul into the cause of protecting our children from the dangers of smoking."[7]

During his Senate career, Gore also became known for his grasp of high-tech issues. He helped to popularize the term *information superhighway*. This refers to the vast potential of personal computers and the Internet to disseminate information. In 1986, Gore sponsored the Supercomputer Network Study Act. The purpose was to explore how to link the nation's supercomputers. Gore also led Congress to ban the sale of human organs and to establish a computer network for organ-transplant donors and recipients.

Gore also became knowledgeable on military issues. Many political analysts said he was a top congressional authority on arms control.[8] Gore served as a liaison between Congress and the Reagan administration as they negotiated agreements on defense issues and arms control with the Soviet Union.

Tipper Gore, meanwhile, was also busy. Besides raising the couple's children, she was pursuing other interests. She earned a master's degree in psychology. She also continued her interest in photography. She volunteered for several organizations to benefit children.

Mrs. Gore was best known for starting a group called the Parents' Music Resource Center (PMRC) in 1984. The purpose of the group was to inform parents about sexual and violent language in popular music. Mrs. Gore was moved to action after she overheard the lyrics to a Prince song on a record belonging to her daughter Karenna.

In 1985, Tipper Gore testified before Congress on the issue. The PMRC proposed warning labels for records that contain violent or sexually explicit material. Mrs. Gore stressed that the labels were voluntary. However, she strongly believed parents needed help in protecting their children from dangerous messages. Mrs. Gore eventually wrote a best-selling book on the subject, *Raising PG Kids in an X-Rated Society*.

The PMRC had much public support, and many record companies agreed to carry the warning labels. Nevertheless, Mrs. Gore and the PMRC attracted controversy. Some people believed Mrs. Gore was calling for censorship and unnecessary government intrusion into people's lives. Frank Zappa called Tipper a "cultural terrorist."[9]

"My first reaction when she started to get involved

in this was, 'Please don't do this,'" Al Gore recalled. "And she convinced me on two different points: No. 1, that it was very different from the image that I had in mind. And No. 2, the remedy she was proposing in no way infringed on the First Amendment, in fact involved no government action of any kind whatsoever." He added, "I'm really very proud of what she has done."[10]

Early in 1987, political analysts began discussing potential candidates for the 1988 presidential race. It was an exciting opportunity for the Democrats: The incumbent president, Ronald Reagan, had served two terms and was not eligible to run again. Reagan, a Republican, had been elected in 1980 and again in 1984. His vice president, George Bush, was the likely Republican candidate in 1988.

Al Gore was among several Democrats mentioned as possible candidates. Conservative commentator John McLaughlin called Gore "too good to be true."[11] Few actually expected him to enter the race, however. First, Gore was young, not even forty years old. Also, despite his accomplishments, he was relatively unknown outside his home state of Tennessee.

Two developments motivated Gore to join the race. First, several well-known politicians declared they would not run. Those potential candidates included Senator Sam Nunn of Georgia, Senator Dale Bumpers of Arkansas, and Governor Mario Cuomo of New York. Then, in the spring of 1987, Gore was approached by a group of Democratic fund-raisers. They assured him that if he ran for office, he would receive their financial backing. "If Al Gore runs," one of the members said, "he will be a well-financed candidate with strong support."[12] Another in the group said, "If he doesn't get the [nomination], he is the obvious running mate for any [candidate]. . . . Al Gore would bring all the necessary pieces."[13]

But Gore was not going to get in the race to wind up number two. He was going to devote his efforts to becoming the Democratic nominee for president. Gore declared himself a candidate. The new candidate's father, Al Gore, Sr., was ecstatic. "I had ambitions for the Presidency—it didn't turn out that way," he said. "I've been negotiating with the Lord to let me live to see that something like that happens [to my son]. But I haven't been able to get a commitment yet."[14]

So it was that Al Gore, Jr., entered his first presidential race. In a speech declaring his candidacy, Gore said the main focuses of his campaign would be global warming, ozone depletion, the ailing worldwide environment, and nuclear arms control.[15] "I know exactly what needs to be done," he added, "and I am impatient to do it."[16] Would he be able to persuade the voters?

Failure and Heartache

Intelligent, meticulous, detail-oriented, ambitious. All of these adjectives are used to describe Al Gore, Jr. People who know him best also say he is sly and funny, with an offbeat sense of humor. In fact, Tipper Gore has said one of the qualities that first attracted her to Al was his wit. "The Al Gore you don't see is a great tease, a lot of fun," said one longtime friend.[1] Yet Gore rarely, if ever, lets the public see this side of him. So he is also described as stiff, formal, even boring and arrogant.

His image was not the only problem Gore faced as he began his quest for the presidency in 1987. The field of Democratic candidates was crowded. Gary Hart, a senator from Colorado, had been considered the front-runner. He dropped out of the race in May

1987 after newspapers reported an extramarital affair. Other candidates in the race were Governor Michael Dukakis of Massachusetts, Representative Richard Gephardt of Missouri, Senator Paul Simon of Illinois, Governor Bruce Babbitt of Arizona, and civil rights leader Jesse Jackson. According to a University of North Carolina poll, Gore was the least known of the candidates. (One magazine reported the results of another, highly unscientific poll. A foreign couple who knew nothing about American politics was shown photos of the Democratic contenders. They chose Gore as looking the most presidential.)[2]

Gore also faced problems because of his wife's work with the Parents' Music Resource Center. Many people believed Tipper Gore's call for warning labels on record albums with explicit lyrics amounted to censorship. Tipper Gore insisted she was against censorship, but political observers said that her activism could have an effect on her husband's success with younger voters.[3]

The Democratic candidates held several debates. Gore, seeking to break out of the pack, tried to portray the other Democrats as weak on foreign policy. At a debate in Des Moines, Iowa, candidate Paul Simon asked Gore to defend his support for the B-1 bomber, the MX missile, and two new aircraft carriers, among other things. "The question itself is part of the problem we face as a Democratic party," Gore replied. "The American people have been given the impression over the last several presidential elections that the Democratic Party is against every weapons system that is suggested and is prepared to go into negotiations

Tipper Gore campaigned successfully for warning labels on popular music with offensive lyrics.

with the Soviet Union on the basis that we get something for nothing."[4]

Gore declared himself a "raging moderate," liberal on domestic issues and conservative on foreign policy. His strategy angered many Democrats who believed there were no significant differences among the candidates. Simon said Gore was "knifing" his opponents. Gephardt said Gore was manufacturing "phony differences."[5]

Gore's numbers rose in the polls. He continued the attacks. Dukakis, Gore said, "doesn't have a single day of foreign-policy experience." Gephardt is a "flip-flopper [who] completely reverses position after position." Jackson, Gore said, "hasn't got a single day of experience in government at any level."[6]

Gore received mixed reviews in the media. Many analysts praised his mastery of complicated issues, rapport with voters, and honesty when he revealed that he had smoked marijuana during his college and Vietnam days.[7] Others, however, said Gore was not tough enough and that although he was a good debater, he was a rotten campaigner.[8]

Gore's family supported him enthusiastically. At his son's request, Al Gore, Sr., stayed on the sidelines when Gore Jr. ran for his first political office. Now he stumped enthusiastically. "I've been through thirty-five states, and I have thirteen to go," said Gore Sr., who was eighty years old at the time.[9] Pauline Gore gave her son words of encouragement. Before one debate, she handed him a note. It stated, "Smile, Relax, Attack."[10]

The "Super Tuesday" primaries were on March 8,

1988. On that day, registered Democratics in twenty states voted for the delegate supporting their favorite candidate. The candidate with the most delegate votes after the primaries was assured the nomination for president at the Democratic National Convention in the summer. Gore knew it was an important day. If he did well, he could win the nomination.

When the results were tallied, Dukakis won the most delegate votes. Gore made a good showing, earning the most delegate votes in six states. Some candidates dropped out of the race, but Gore kept going.

Then came the New York primary. This, too, was another important vote. Gore asked New York City Mayor Ed Koch to campaign with him. This turned out to be a mistake. Koch, a colorful and controversial figure, made disparaging remarks about African-American Jesse Jackson. Koch said Jews would be crazy to vote for Jackson. He also accused Jackson of lying.[11] Koch's remarks offended many people, and Gore was guilty by association. Gore did poorly in the primary.

"I had plenty of options," Gore said later. "None of them were very attractive. I felt that was the appropriate response, to make it clear that [Koch] was speaking for himself and not me, and that I did not agree with what he was saying but I was grateful for his endorsement of my candidacy. The fact that a particular option doesn't work well doesn't always mean that there's another that'll work a lot better."[12]

After the New York primary, Gore realized that he never would be able to muster enough support. He dropped out of the presidential race. Some political analysts praised a "classy withdrawal" and said they hoped that Gore would learn from his mistakes and return to the presidential arena.[13]

At the Democratic National Convention in the summer of 1988, Michael Dukakis was officially nominated as the presidential candidate. That fall, he and his running mate, Senator Lloyd Bentsen, were soundly beaten. American voters elected Republican George Bush as president and Dan Quayle as vice president.

Gore's experience as a national candidate was disappointing. But a tragic incident two years later put the loss into perspective. One afternoon in April 1989, Al and Tipper Gore took their son, Albert III, to a baseball game in Baltimore, Maryland. As they were leaving, the six-year-old boy shook loose from his father and ran into the street. Little Albert was struck by a car and thrown thirty feet into the air. He landed in a gutter and was severely injured, with broken ribs, a broken leg, and crushed internal organs. He was in a coma for several days. When Albert regained consciousness, he told his parents, "I can't get well without you."[14]

Gore's son spent three months at Johns Hopkins Hospital in Baltimore, slowly recovering from his injuries. For the first month, Gore moved into his son's room. He watched the boy around the clock. "It was a terrible jolt for Al, a defining moment," a friend recalled. "Al hasn't been the same since."[15] "For Al, there was tremendous guilt that he should have been watching [Al III] more closely," another friend said. "With Tipper, it was anger. It's very tough on a marriage to go through this stuff."[16]

While camping out at the hospital, Gore began thinking about his life. He was forty years old. He had suffered defeat in a presidential primary. His son had nearly died. He felt he had lost touch with himself as well as with his family. One particular regret was that during the 1988 campaign, he had practically abandoned the environmental issues that were so dear to him. He had been persuaded that voters were not interested. "I began to doubt my own political judgment, so I began to ask the pollsters and professional politicians what they thought I ought to talk about," he later said. "As a result, for much of the campaign I discussed what everybody else discussed, which too often was a familiar list of what insiders agree are 'the issues.'"[17]

Gore began writing a book, *Earth in the Balance*, which describes his environmental views. He later said he wrote the book "to fully search my heart and mind about this challenge to which I feel called—and in the process to summon the courage to make a full and unreserved commitment to see it through."[18] The book, which was published in 1992, became a best-seller.

"When you've seen your six-year-old son fighting for his life, you realize that some things matter a lot more than winning," Gore said in a speech a few years later. "You lose patience with the lazy assumption of so many in politics that we can always just muddle through. When you've seen your reflection in the empty stare of a boy waiting for his second breath of life, you realize that we were not put here on earth to look out for our needs alone."[19]

When Al Gore III finally returned home, he was in a full-body cast. He continued to need intensive therapy and care. Tipper and Al set up their son's bed in the dining room of their Arlington home. "We gave each of his sisters a role in his recovery," Tipper later recalled. "Albert had to be turned regularly each night during this period, and the children took turns staying up with him so Al and I could get some sleep."[20] Eventually, Al Gore III made a full recovery.

"It was a shattering experience for our whole family," Al Gore, Jr., recalled. "And yet it has been in so many ways a great blessing for us. I never thought at the time I'd ever be able to say that. It completely changed my outlook on life."[21]

Later, Gore revealed that his family sought counseling to help them deal with their experience. In a time when many people equated seeking counseling with being unstable, it was a brave admission. "We grew tremendously by becoming aware of how we were dealing with it and how we were relating to one another in the midst of it," Gore said. "I strongly recommend to any family . . . not to be afraid to do this."[22]

Gore's experiences taught him that he could no longer take family for granted. Running for president had been a time-consuming job; he had frequently been absent from his family. His daughters were growing up and leaving for college. His son had just been through a terrible ordeal. Tipper missed and needed her husband. So in 1991, Gore announced that he would not run for president in 1992. He did not say anything about sitting out a race for vice president, however.

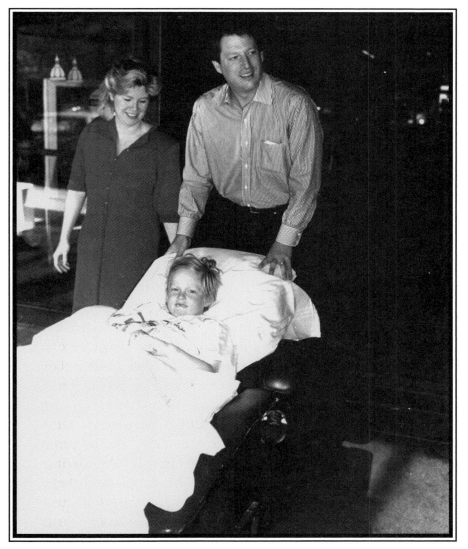

"I can't get well without you," six-year-old Albert III told his parents after he was hit by a car. He left the hospital in a full-body cast.

Back in the Race

Actually, Al Gore, Jr., did not plan to run for either president or vice president in the 1992 election. The issue of the vice presidency first came up when Gore was running for president in 1988. Some political analysts said he was too young and too little known to get elected president. They thought he should run for vice president. The position would be a good training ground for the presidency. Gore did not agree. "I'm not interested," he said then, "and I'm not kidding."[1]

Shortly after his defeat in the 1988 primary, Gore had briefly considered trying again for the 1992 bid. After his son's accident, he changed his mind. He realized his family needed him. A presidential campaign would take too much time and energy. Gore did want to remain in politics, however. He was reelected to the Senate in 1990.

In the summer of 1991, Gore formally announced that he would not run for the nation's highest office. "I would like to be president," he said, "but I am also a father, and I feel deeply about my responsibility to my children."[2]

Other well-known politicians, including Governor Mario Cuomo of New York and Senator Bill Bradley of New Jersey, announced they would not run, either. Indeed, few were eager to take on President George Bush. He had just successfully commanded the Persian Gulf War. In August 1990, Iraq had invaded a neighboring country, oil-rich Kuwait. The United States and some other United Nations member countries became concerned about the availability of oil. They immediately sent forces to protect Saudi Arabia and other Arab countries from possible invasion. This military action was called Operation Desert Shield.

Bush gave Iraqi leader Saddam Hussein a January 1991 deadline for leaving Kuwait. Saddam refused to remove his troops, and Operation Desert Shield became Operation Desert Storm. Through air and then ground attacks, the American-led forces handily beat the Iraqi troops. There were few injuries and deaths to American service members. Kuwait was liberated, and the war was over by March 1991. Americans were impressed with Bush's decisiveness. His popularity rating soared to 91 percent, one of the highest of any American president in history.

The Democrats who declared themselves presidential candidates included former Massachusetts senator Paul Tsongas, Virginia governor L. Douglas Wilder, and former California governor Jerry Brown. Billionaire businessman H. Ross Perot also entered the race as an independent candidate. Many political analysts and Democrats believed that if Gore changed his mind, he would be the man to beat. They said he was the obvious favorite because he had run before. His failed candidacy was now seen as a good learning experience. Also, Gore had a spotless private life that had withstood the investigation that comes with being a candidate.[3] Despite this positive feedback, Gore still refused to enter the race.

In October 1991, another politician declared himself a candidate. He was Arkansas governor Bill Clinton. Like Gore, Clinton considered himself a New Democrat. Traditionally, Democrats had the reputation of spending too much money on social causes and of being too liberal on economic and military issues. New Democrats said they cared about social policies but also believed in more conservative economic and defense policies.

From the beginning, Clinton was a controversial candidate. When he had been elected to his fifth term as governor the previous year, he had promised Arkansas voters he would not seek higher office. Clinton also faced character issues. He was accused of having extramarital affairs, avoiding the draft during the Vietnam War, and smoking marijuana. The concern was not only that he may have done those things but that he had not told the complete truth. For example, when he finally admitted smoking marijuana, he added, "but I didn't inhale." That line became a national joke.

Despite these problems, Clinton slowly emerged as the leading Democratic contender. In debates among the candidates, he proved to be knowledgeable and personable. Clinton also found an issue that appealed to the voters: the economy. When he ran for president in 1988, Bush had promised the American voters: "Read my lips: No new taxes." This slogan helped get Bush elected. But he went back on his promise. With the economy faltering, Bush approved a tax-increase plan. By the middle of 1992, Bush's popularity rating had fallen below 30 percent. The seemingly unbeatable incumbent president suddenly looked vulnerable.

By June 1992, Clinton had earned enough delegate votes in the primaries to win the Democratic nomination for president the following month. Now it was time to choose a running mate. Warren Christopher, a lawyer who was in charge of Clinton's search for a vice president, drafted a list of names. He met with several Democrats to get their opinions. Christopher set up a meeting with Gore. According to Christopher, Gore spoke highly about several of the candidates. Toward the end of the conversation, Christopher asked Gore if he was interested in the job.[4]

"It was a very guarded, reluctant response," Christopher recalled. "He said that was something he would have to think about for a long time."[5] A month later, Christopher had whittled the list down to a few names. These candidates would personally meet with Clinton. Christopher called Gore and asked if he would meet with Clinton. Gore asked for a day to think it over.

"I thought about it," Gore later said. "I reframed the question to take the personal ambition part out of it, because I didn't want to do it in that sense. I didn't expect it. I didn't seek it."[6] Gore added that he did not ask himself if he wanted to run for vice president. He asked himself, "Were you willing to give your country a better chance to change?" The answer was yes.[7]

Gore also talked with his wife and children. He had intended to stay out of the race for his family's sake. But Tipper reminded him that running for vice president would last only a few months, since the election was in November. Tipper worried about the children. She did not want them feeling "insecure or intruded upon," she said.[8] At the same time, Tipper thought her husband actually might have more time to spend with his family if he were vice president. As a senator, he made weekly trips to Tennessee to meet with his constituents. "We talked a lot about what our life would be like if we won, and we thought it would be more manageable in many ways," Mrs. Gore said.[9]

Perhaps most important, Tipper believed her husband would make a great vice president. She felt he would be a "voice for change, to offer leadership toward a whole range of domestic goals we thought had been ignored."[10] So with Albert III healed from his accident and the Gore family ties renewed, Tipper gave Al her support.

Gore met with Clinton at the end of June in 1992. The two men had met only once before, five years earlier. At that time, it was Gore who was running for president. Gore had met with Clinton to seek his support. They had gotten along well and realized they had much in common. Besides similar political views, they were both southerners and from the same generation.

In his book *The Agenda: Inside the Clinton White House*, investigative reporter Bob Woodward (of Watergate fame) described the Clinton-Gore meeting. Clinton had spent the day at a hotel in Washington, interviewing potential vice presidential candidates. Gore arrived late in the day. They spent three hours talking. Gore told Clinton that he was not seeking the nomination but would happily accept it.[11]

Gore also told Clinton that if they were elected, he wanted an active role in running the country. Historically, the vice presidency is a largely symbolic job. In fact, the vice president's only power spelled out in the Constitution is to preside over the Senate and break tie votes. As John Adams, the nation's first vice president, wrote to his wife, Abigail: "My country has in its wisdom contrived for me the most insignificant office that ever the invention of man contrived or his imagination conceived . . . I can do neither good nor evil."[12]

Clinton promised Gore important roles in Gore's favorite areas: the environment, technology, and national security.[13] He also said he and Gore would meet on a regular basis. Gore's desire to be more than a figurehead impressed Clinton. After they met, Clinton told one of his advisers that he preferred Gore over the other candidates because he and Gore communicated well. When the aide asked for another reason, Clinton said, "I could die, that's why."[14] In other words, Clinton thought Gore would be able to take over as president if necessary.

Clinton also received information from a close

The Clintons and the Gores decided to join forces for the 1992 presidential race.

friend of Gore's. The friend said Gore had intelligence and stamina. "And most importantly he won't stab you in the back," the friend said, "even if you deserve it."[15] The next day, Clinton announced that he had selected Al Gore as his vice presidential running mate.

The Clinton-Gore ticket generated immediate excitement. "In an age when it is supposed to be bad to be a politician, they are boomers who decided . . . to join up, to become part of the system in order to change it," one political columnist wrote. "They are both self-created and both highly motivated public-issues people. . . . They are ambitious, motivated, determined, political, government-minded people."[16]

In July 1992, at Madison Square Garden in New

York City, the Democrats officially nominated Bill Clinton and Al Gore as their candidates for president and vice president. Gore, usually described as unemotional and stiff in public, impressed the crowd with his personal and moving acceptance speech. With photos of his son projected behind him, Gore described Albert III's near-fatal accident and long recovery. He compared his son's healing with the healing he hoped to bring to the country. He said:

> *All of us are part of something much greater than we are capable of imagining. And, my friends, if you look up for a moment from the rush of your daily lives, you will hear the quiet voices of your country crying out for help. You will see your reflection in the weary eyes of those who are losing hope in America. And you will see that our democracy is lying there in the gutter waiting for us to give it a second breath of life.*
>
> *I don't care what party you're in, whether you're an Independent, whether you have been tempted to just give up completely on the whole political process, we want you to join this common effort to unite our country behind a higher calling.*[17]

After Gore's speech, it was Clinton's turn to speak. "I am so *proud* of Al Gore," he said.[18]

The nomination process had been tough for Clinton. He emerged the victor in the delegate count but did not have a majority of public support. He had received only about 30 percent of the votes cast in the primaries.[19] Clinton's selection of Gore as a running mate had caused Clinton's poll numbers to rise. Still, he trailed behind both Bush and Perot. Clearly, the two Democrats had their work cut out for them.

"Excellent Adventure"

Shortly after the Democratic convention, the two candidates and their wives left for a campaign bus tour across parts of America. They spent grueling, fourteen-hour days meeting people and asking for votes. The tour tired them, but it also energized them. Bill Clinton and Al Gore got to know each other as friends and political partners. The two forty-something, attractive southerners, with their pretty, blond, modern wives, generated much enthusiasm. The press nicknamed the bus tour "Al and Bill's Excellent Adventure," after a popular teen movie.

The campaign was hard work, but the candidates also found time for fun. Bill Clinton played his saxophone on *The Arsenio Hall Show*, a late-night television program popular among younger viewers. He also fielded questions from young voters on MTV, the cable television music channel. Tipper Gore once chased after reporters with water pistols. She also played a joke on her husband. While he was being interviewed on the television show *Larry King Live*, she phoned in to the program. "You're the most handsome man I've ever seen," she told Al, disguising her voice. Gore was embarrassed. King reminded the caller that Gore was happily married and not available for a date. "Not even with his wife?" asked Tipper, laughing.[1]

Everywhere the candidates went, they described their vision for America. The basement of the governor's mansion in Little Rock, Arkansas, served as headquarters for the Clinton–Gore campaign. Hillary Clinton called it "The War Room." There, a sign on the wall reminded the candidates of their focus:

> CHANGE VS. MORE OF THE SAME.
> THE ECONOMY, STUPID.
> DON'T FORGET HEALTH CARE.[2]

During the bus tour, Gore sharpened his speaking skills. His routine was to greet the crowd, then list failures of the current administration. "Bush and Quayle have run out of ideas," he would conclude. "They've run out of energy. They've run out of gas, and with your help come November, they're going to be run out of office!"

Gore would add, "It's time for Bush and Quayle to go!" and then ask the crowd, "What time is it?" The crowd always roared back, "It's time for them to go!"[3]

Gore's primary focus was the environment. He

Al and Tipper Gore work hard to make the world a better place—through both politics and social activism.

had abandoned the subject in his 1988 race for the presidency. He would not do that again. Even before he and Clinton began campaigning together, Gore made it clear the environment was his top priority. One time in Little Rock, aides gave Clinton and Gore a mock briefing. Anticipating that Gore's views could cause controversy with some voters, one aide asked Gore if he was an environmental extremist. Gore replied by reciting sections of his book *Earth in the Balance.* "That was a really good answer," Clinton told him. "But we need to come at it a little different. I don't think we want to come across as Greenpeace warriors." Gore retorted, "What do you mean we, kemo sabe?"[4]

On the campaign trail, Gore spoke frequently about the topic he cared so much about. "I have emphasized the environment more than any other issue in this campaign," he said. "I have designed my schedule in a way that helps me highlight the environment at as many stops as possible."[5]

Part of Gore's commitment to stress the environment stemmed from his disappointment with the Bush administration's performance during the Earth Summit. The summit, officially called the United Nations Conference on Environment and Development, was held in June 1992 in Rio de Janeiro, Brazil. Gore headed the Senate delegation to the summit. The summit marked the first time leaders from around the world met to discuss environmental concerns.

In his book *Earth in the Balance*, Gore said the summit was a success for the world as a whole, but not for the United States. "Our nation found itself embarrassed and isolated," he said. "The Bush

Al Gore with actor Christopher Reeve, right, and members of Clean Ocean Action at the annual beach cleanup in Sandy Hook, New Jersey, in 1992.

administration insisted that our delegation argue in favor of so many nonsensical positions that a deadlock was virtually guaranteed."[6] Gore specifically mentioned that other countries were willing to set targets for reducing emissions of carbon dioxide, but Bush officials insisted the targets were not necessary. The United States "not only failed to lead but actively fought against needed progress on the environment," Gore wrote.[7]

The Republican candidates ridiculed Gore for his environmental focus. President Bush called him "Ozone Man." Vice President Dan Quayle said Gore was an extremist. In response, Gore told *Time* magazine:

> *I believe that the extremist view is held by those who are willing to tolerate the doubling of carbon dioxide in a single generation, the loss in a single lifetime of more than half the living species God put on earth, the destruction of a large percentage of the protective ozone shield in only a few decades, the loss of more than an acre of tropical rain forest every second . . . the poisoning of our air and water resources, the serious erosion of our cropland.*[8]

As the November election grew closer, independent candidate Ross Perot, who had dropped out, reentered the race. He had lost much of his support, however, and the Democrats' momentum did not slow. Many people believed that having Gore on the ticket saved Clinton's campaign. Gore's experience in Washington, strong marriage, service in Vietnam, and even support for the Persian Gulf War were seen as pluses for the Democratic ticket.[9]

Others believed that Gore's presence highlighted Vice President Quayle's shortcomings. Quayle, a congressman from Indiana, had been a controversial choice when Bush chose him as running mate in 1988. Quayle was young and relatively unknown. He had not built a record of accomplishments in Washington. Also, during the Vietnam War, Quayle had stayed in the United States, serving in the National Guard. Quayle's prominent family had worked behind the scenes to get Quayle into the guard so he would not have to fight in Vietnam.

After being elected vice president in 1988, Quayle helped Bush with foreign trade issues and the space program, among other things. Yet he was unable to shake his lightweight image. He mispronounced words and bungled sayings. His blunders were prominently displayed in the media. For example, one time he visited an elementary school classroom. With television cameras rolling, Quayle approached a boy who had written the word *potato* on the chalkboard. Quayle incorrectly told the boy he had spelled "potato" wrong. The vice president added an *e*, changing the spelling to *potatoe*.

Before the 1992 election, several Republicans urged Bush to take Quayle off the ticket and choose another running mate. Bush refused, but the Republican candidates usually campaigned separately. Now Quayle was being unfavorably compared with Gore. "Gore has written a book," said one Democratic senator, "and Quayle can't spell."[10] "Both of the Democratic candidates are young and smart," said one Republican campaign official, "and we've only got one of each."[11]

In a poll conducted a month before the election, *Newsweek* asked voters whom they would choose if they could vote separately for vice president. Gore received 61 percent of the vote. Quayle received only 28 percent, and James Stockdale, the independent candidate who was running with Ross Perot, received 6 percent.[12]

Other polls showed that even among Republicans, a majority preferred Gore over Quayle. That same month, *Time* magazine asked Gore why voters should care who was vice president. After all, the second-in-command position was not historically an important one. "There have been many times in our nation's history when the vice president has suddenly been thrust into the presidency owing to an unanticipated death or tragedy," Gore replied. "Secondly, Bill Clinton and I have a shared understanding of what the words partnership and teamwork are all about."[13]

Tipper Gore was also seen as a boost to the Democratic ticket. Hillary Clinton was a lawyer who continued to hold high-powered jobs during her husband's political career. She was criticized by many for being a working mom. When she defended herself as someone who did not just stay home and bake cookies, she offended many people. Tipper Gore, on the other hand, was described as a "crusading homemaker."[14] Her work to provide warning labels for explicit music lyrics proved she cared about families. "In a funny way [Tipper's] almost a godsend for Governor Clinton," said one political insider. "She is so proper and so closely identified with the values system."[15]

Even the Gore kids got in on the act. They accompanied their parents on many campaign stops. Albert III reportedly was the most enthusiastic of the children, shaking hands and even signing autographs. But when he turned ten years old on October 19, all the Gores took a break from the race to enjoy a private celebration.

The Democrats encountered some rough spots during the presidential race. During one vice presidential debate, Quayle attacked Clinton's character. Some of Clinton's advisers later thought that Gore could have said more to defend Clinton. Gore was also criticized for his public-speaking style. Many agreed he was more animated than he had been in the 1988 race, but he still tended to be wooden and stiff. His friends told reporters that they wished he would show his humorous side.

Still, on the first Tuesday in November 1992, when the American voters went to the polls, the Democrats came out on top. Independent candidate Ross Perot earned 19 percent of the vote. The incumbent, George Bush, received 38 percent. Bill Clinton, who was called the "Comeback Kid" for his ability to survive political turmoil, was elected president. He received 43 percent of the popular vote.

Clinton's victory meant that the Gores would be leaving the house in Arlington, Virginia, where they had spent the past sixteen years. The next stop: the vice president's residence at the Naval Observatory, and a job that Gore once said he had neither sought nor expected.

The First
Four Years

When he won the election in
1992, Bill Clinton was one of the youngest men ever
to become president of the United States. He was also
the first Democrat elected to the White House since
Jimmy Carter won the presidency in 1976. Vice
President Al Gore had his own notable first, but it
did not become obvious until his term was nearly
completed. Gore became one of the first vice presidents
to elevate the position beyond the ceremonial. He
became one of the most influential vice presidents in
the history of the country. "I believe," Clinton said
later, "based on everything I've been able to read or
learn from others, he [Gore] has a larger role
substantively and more influence than any Vice
President. Ever."[1]

Back in 1992, Gore had concerns about the job of vice president. He did not want to be merely a symbolic leader. Clinton had promised Gore that if they were elected, Gore would play a key role in issues concerning the environment, technology, and national security. "Watch Al," said one adviser. "Al will figure out a way to be important."[2]

Gore had other requests. He wanted to meet with Clinton weekly for lunch. He wanted an office at the White House that was close to the president's Oval Office. Gore also wanted his chief of staff to be a presidential assistant as well. That way, the two staffs would be able to coordinate their activities better. Clinton agreed to all of Gore's requests.

Shortly after the November 1992 election, the new vice president temporarily moved to Little Rock, Arkansas. There, Clinton and a team of advisers were making plans for the new administration. Gore got up early every morning and went jogging with the president-elect. Then, he and other advisers met with Clinton to discuss Cabinet posts and other high-level appointments. Gore played a big role in some appointments. For example, he disagreed with Clinton's choice for head of the Environmental Protection Agency. Gore preferred his former Senate aide, Carol Browner, for the job. She got it. Gore recommended economist Laura Tyson to head the Council of Economic Advisers, and she was chosen.

Clinton and Gore were sworn into office in January 1993. Gore's first major assignment was to take on the task of "reinventing" government. Ross Perot's run for president had revealed that many

Americans had become frustrated with the federal government. They felt little was being accomplished and that taxpayer dollars were being wasted. Clinton wanted to reach out to these voters. Gore's assignment was to study the workings of the federal government and to devise a plan to improve it. Clinton promised Gore that he would support his efforts and work to get his plan implemented.

Gore took on the task with his usual attention to detail. He formed a committee, set up meetings, and thoroughly studied the issue. He also talked to government workers. Gore was astonished by the examples of waste and mismanagement. "A federal worker told me

After the election, the Gore family moved into Admiralty House, the official vice presidential home on the grounds of the United States Naval Observatory.

that twenty-three separate people had to sign off on one requisition for a PC [personal computer]," Gore said. "So, it's a whole dysfunctional system."[3]

By September 1993, Gore's plan for reinventing government, or ReGo, was ready. He titled it "From Red Tape to Results: Creating a Government That Works Better and Costs Less." Gore's plan called for eliminating thousands of government jobs to save money. The plan also gave individual government agencies the power to hire and promote workers based on the agencies' own procedures. It required the agencies to measure their programs' effectiveness. Previously, only the amount of work employees completed had been measured.

Gore's plan also permitted national parks to raise fees to cover their costs. It provided incentives for agencies to save money and gave managers more flexibility to train and reward workers.[4]

To generate public support and enthusiasm for his project, Gore appeared on the television program *Late Night with David Letterman*. It was Gore's idea to go on the show. His aides met with producers. They wanted to make sure Gore did not appear undignified. A producer on the show told him, "Here's the opportunity to show people you have a sense of humor."[5]

Gore performed in a Stupid Government Tricks skit, which was a variation of Letterman's Stupid Pet Tricks. In the skit, the vice president ridiculed complicated federal rules for purchasing common items such as ashtrays and floor wax. Gore also wrote his own Top Ten List. His was titled, "Ten Good Things About Being Vice President." One of his favorites was

At the far left are Clinton and Gore at the swearing-in of new Cabinet members. Al Gore played a big role in the selection of Cabinet members for Clinton's administration.

"If you close your left eye, the seal on the podium reads, 'President of the United States.'"[6] Gore's performance was widely praised. For the moment, his wooden image was erased.

Two months later, Gore was on national television again. This time, he went face-to-face with Ross Perot on CNN's *Larry King Live*. The two debated the merits of the North American Free Trade Agreement (NAFTA).

Perot had announced his candidacy for the presidency on *Larry King Live* in early 1992. His platform was to reduce the size of government and to reform it. Millions of people rallied to his cause. Perot was defeated, but he earned an impressive number of votes. He vowed to continue to play a role in politics. Perot formed a group called United We Stand America.

In November 1993, Congress was preparing to vote on NAFTA. The agreement would eliminate trade barriers between countries in North America. The Clinton administration supported the plan, saying it would lead to more job and investment opportunities. Perot was against NAFTA. He said Americans would lose jobs to foreigners. His often-repeated phrase "giant sucking sound" referred to his fear that American jobs would go to lower-paid Mexican workers.

The president was worried that Perot's criticism would lead Congress to defeat NAFTA. He asked Gore to debate Perot on national television. "Our principal mission was to demonstrate that the stuff Perot has been putting out about NAFTA was garbage," said one of Gore's aides.[7] Gore had only four days to prepare for the televised debate. His aides compiled a thick briefing book. The vice president studied it intently. He reviewed videotapes of Perot's television appearances. He also researched claims Perot was making about NAFTA and came up with rebuttals. He held a mock debate before appearing on the show. Gore later said that he also prayed. "When I'm in a situation like that, I pray about it," he said. "And if there's intense pressure, and I know in my heart it's the right thing, I pray that it will happen as it should, and I just then forget about the outcome and feel confident. And that may sound corny but that's the truth."[8]

Gore's preparation paid off. Point by point, Gore refuted Perot's claims. Perot lost his temper and made a bad impression on viewers. "The Vice President of the United States had to be trained all weekend to be arrogant, condescending and rude," Perot later told reporters.[9] A few days after the television debate, Congress passed NAFTA. Republicans and Democrats alike voted for the plan. Gore was largely responsible for the victory.

No matter what his assignment, Gore was diligent. Yet he also showed his usually private sense of humor. One time, camera crews rearranged the Oval Office before Clinton gave a televised address on the economy. Afterward, Gore helped them put the bust of President Harry Truman back in its correct place. "This is what vice presidents are for," he joked.[10] Another time, Gore gave Clinton a cardboard cutout of himself. He said it was so Clinton would never be without Gore standing a half step behind him.[11]

Gore also played jokes on his wife, Tipper. One time when he was getting ready for an important meeting, he pretended that he had accidentally washed his hair with hair-removal cream instead of shampoo. He laughed loudly when Tipper shrieked in despair.

Gore became one of Clinton's closest advisers. He attended dress rehearsals before Clinton made important speeches, and he critiqued Clinton's performances. He was even known to type in revisions to Clinton's speeches. Gore also made recommendations on the hiring and firing of advisers. "My principal mission is to help Bill Clinton be the most successful president he can be," Gore said. "The only time I speak up is when I feel that the President is not going to be well served by going in the direction that is recommended."[12]

Clinton's advisers appreciated Gore. They felt he had developed a way of talking candidly to Clinton without overstepping his authority. Gore often prefaced his advice by saying, "I hope I'm not offending you," or "I hope I'm not taking advantage of our relationship."[13]

Gore was not afraid to speak out, but the president did not always follow his advice. "I'm not out to win arguments for the sake of winning arguments," Gore once said. "But if some principle is at stake which I think is crucial, then I will push it harder."[14]

Clinton also relied on Gore to help him understand the inner workings of Washington. Gore had been a congressman and a senator, as well as the son of a congressman-turned-senator. As governor of Arkansas, Clinton had no experience with Congress. The new president did not understand many of the behind-the-scenes aspects of getting things done in Washington.

Gore and Clinton got along well despite differences in personal style. Gore was a very disciplined worker; Clinton was more free-form. Clinton was outgoing; Gore was more reserved. Clinton kept late hours; Gore liked to go to bed early. Clinton liked to relax on the golf course; Gore did not.

During his first four years as vice president, Gore compiled an impressive list of accomplishments. He played a key role in a historic deal with the Ukraine. That former Soviet republic agreed to surrender its nuclear warheads. He negotiated with television executives to establish a voluntary ratings system for their programs. He worked with Congress to pass the Telecommunications Act of 1996. This bill lifted restrictions that prevented telephone companies from competing with one another. It also enabled more competition in the cable television industry. Additionally, the bill required the installation of V-chips in new television sets. These chips allow parents to screen out programs they deem unsuitable for their children. The bill also called for fines and jail terms for those who made indecent material available to children through online computer networks. President Clinton called Vice President Gore the father of the groundbreaking new act. Clinton signed it with the pen President Eisenhower used when he signed the bill creating the interstate highway system. That bill had been sponsored by Senator Al Gore, Sr.

Gore was also instrumental in setting up an Internet service called Welcome to the White House: An Interactive Citizens' Handbook. The World Wide Web service provided a single point of access to all government information for the executive branch of the government. Users were able to access information including White House documents, a virtual tour of the White House, and information about Cabinet-level and independent government agencies. The Web site <http://www.whitehouse.gov> included photographs, audio, and links to other government Web sites and services.

Gore also headed the White House campaigns to discourage teen smoking and to strengthen regulation of tobacco products. He led a task force on airline safety after TWA Flight 800 inexplicably exploded in 1996, killing hundreds of people. Gore "reset the bar

Vice President Al Gore, far left, and notable members of Congress look on as President Clinton signs the National Voter Registration Act of 1993.

for measuring the effectiveness of future Vice Presidents," said one political consultant.[15]

Despite his wealth of accomplishments, Gore did not express frustration or dissatisfaction with being second-in-command. "I have never felt what so many vice presidents have reportedly felt: 'That should be me there.' Or 'I could do a lot better,'" Gore said. "And I'm not spending any time or energy thinking about tomorrow and the ambition to be president. Some people might find that implausible, but that's the honest truth."[16]

Gore's achievements were impressive. The Clinton administration as a whole, however, got mixed reviews for its first term. Clinton devised an economic plan that, after a long struggle, was passed by Congress. The plan offered a stronger economy, increased job security, and more opportunities for the middle class.[17] Clinton's national service program was also passed. Yet the Clinton administration failed in one of its top priorities: health care reform. Shortly after taking office, Clinton put his wife, Hillary Rodham Clinton, in charge of health care reform. The goal was to ensure medical care for every American. Mrs. Clinton called together a group of five hundred expert advisers. Worried that the media would print negative stories, she held some meetings in private and did not reveal the names of a few committee members. There was much criticism of Mrs. Clinton's lack of openness, including a lawsuit.[18] Progress on health care reform was delayed. When the health care plan was finally released, it was severely criticized. Congress failed to pass it.

On Election Day in 1994, Democratic candidates fared badly in their House, Senate, and gubernatorial races. It was a clear indication that voters were not happy with Clinton's performance as president. In fact, after his first one hundred days in office, Clinton's approval rating was 55 percent. President Carter's had been at 63 percent. Reagan's had been at 68 percent.

The Clintons also had personal upheavals during their first term in office. Mrs. Clinton's father suffered a stroke and died. Deputy White House Counsel Vincent Foster committed suicide. He had been a personal friend of both Clintons. Also, the Whitewater investigation unfolded. The Clintons were accused by some Republicans of being involved in shady real estate and investment dealings when Clinton was governor of Arkansas.

Shortly after the Whitewater story broke, Clinton's mother, Virginia Kelley, died. Senate Majority Leader Bob Dole, a Republican, went on national television to praise Mrs. Kelley. Then, he started talking about the Whitewater investigation. He demanded that a special prosecutor look into the Clintons' business dealings.

Dole continued to speak out about Whitewater, even as Clinton was attending his mother's funeral service. Gore went on television and asked Dole to give Clinton a break. "Now doesn't it bother you a little bit to have the president attending the funeral service of his mother," Gore said, "and to have members of the political opposition, as the service is going on . . . making these attacks?"[19]

By 1995, Clinton began thinking about the presidential race of 1996. It had been a rough few years as president, but he wanted to serve another term. There was still so much he wanted to accomplish. Clinton knew he could not do it without Al Gore. There was no doubt that Clinton would keep Gore as his second-in-command.

Four More Years

Toward the end of his first term, things were not going well for President Clinton, professionally or personally. Professionally, he had not accomplished all he had wanted to as president. Personally, his private life was under attack. Independent prosecutor Kenneth Starr was investigating Hillary and Bill Clinton's role in the Whitewater real estate deal. Also, a lawsuit had been brought against the president. Paula Jones, a former Arkansas state employee, claimed that in 1991, Clinton, who was governor of Arkansas, had made unwanted sexual advances. In May 1994, she filed a sexual harassment lawsuit against him. It was the first time a civil suit had been filed against a sitting president for something that occurred before he took office. With all that was happening, how could Clinton muster the energy to campaign for reelection?

As he often did when he had a problem to discuss or a big decision to make, Clinton turned to his vice president. Al Gore had become one of Clinton's most trusted advisers. The two men had agreed to get together regularly if they were elected the leaders of the United States. Now, both men had come to look forward to their weekly lunch date. It was a chance to relax and reconnect.

In early 1995, during one of their lunches, Clinton asked Gore his opinion of their first term. Gore said he believed Clinton had tried to please too many people instead of taking a firm stand and sticking to it. Gore said Clinton needed to ask himself a question: "What do I want?" Clinton said he wanted his presidency back.[1]

Clinton and Gore began meeting regularly with political advisers to discuss election strategy, personnel, and advertising. Gore was credited with helping Clinton become more disciplined and focused, with both the campaign and the presidency. Gore recommended people for important jobs, not only with the reelection effort but also on the White House staff.

As part of campaigning, Gore made telephone calls asking for monetary contributions. Between December 1995 and May 1996, he made about one phone call every two days, according to one analysis. Gore also attended political fund-raisers. In April 1996, Gore attended a fund-raiser at a Buddhist temple near Los Angeles. Asking for donations and attending fund-raisers were part of running for office. But these acts soon would land Gore in trouble.

Clinton, meanwhile, realized he was running not only for himself but also for Al Gore's political future. If the Democrats were reelected in 1996, Gore would be the natural candidate for president in the year 2000. For Gore's birthday in March 1996, Clinton gave Gore fake keys to Air Force One, the presidential plane. He also gave his vice president a photo of the two of them at a State of the Union Address. Their faces were reversed to make it appear as though Gore were the president and Clinton, the vice president.

As the presidential primaries grew closer, several Republicans announced they would challenge Bill Clinton for the presidency. The candidates included former Tennessee governor Lamar Alexander, Texas senator Phil Gramm, and publisher Steve Forbes. The early favorite was Senate Majority Leader Bob Dole. Dole, from Kansas, was in his early seventies. He had served in Congress for more than thirty years. He was Gerald Ford's vice presidential running mate in 1976, when they were defeated by Jimmy Carter and Walter Mondale. Dole challenged Ronald Reagan for the presidential nomination in 1980. He challenged George Bush in 1988. Both times, Dole failed.

Dole had a gruff personality and a habit of talking about himself in the third person, as in "Bob Dole thinks this." He is a veteran of World War II who was severely injured in battle and no longer has the use of his right arm. His wife, Elizabeth Dole, is a lawyer. She held Cabinet posts in both the Reagan and Bush administrations and then became president of the American Red Cross, a post she held until 1999.

After struggling with Forbes in the primaries, Dole emerged as the Republican candidate. He resigned from the Senate to devote all his energy to the presidential race. For his running mate, he chose Jack Kemp, a former congressman and secretary of Housing and Urban Development. Dole said he wanted a running mate who would be a partner in leadership, similar to Clinton and Gore's arrangement. "Very frankly, I think Vice President Gore was pretty well picked," Dole said. "In fact, I'm surprised at how the vice president interrupts, takes over, even in the budget discussions . . . which I think wouldn't bother me. I'm used to staff people interrupting me."[2]

Along with playing a major role in the reelection campaign, Gore continued to be influential in leading the country. For example, Gore tried to persuade Clinton to take stronger action in Bosnia. Civil war had been raging for years among three different factions in that part of the former Yugoslavia. Horror stories were being reported about ethnic-cleansing techniques that included mass rape and murder. The events were being likened to the Holocaust, when German leader Adolf Hitler tried to rid the world of Jews and other groups of people he considered inferior.

United Nations forces were sent to Bosnia as peacekeepers. But they were ineffective, and the war raged on. In July 1996, *The Washington Post* and other newspapers ran a photo of a young refugee woman. Full of despair over the war, she had killed herself. "My 21-year-old daughter asked me about that picture," Gore told the president. "What am I supposed to tell her? Why is this happening and we're not doing anything?"[3]

"My daughter is surprised the world is allowing this to happen," Gore added. "I am too."[4] Eventually, United Nations forces began bombing raids. Then, President Clinton's United Nations representative, Bill Richardson, was able to persuade leaders of the warring factions to meet. A peace conference was held in Dayton, Ohio. The leaders agreed to cease fighting.

In the summer of 1996, Democrats gathered in Chicago for their national convention. Some politicians previously had thoughts of challenging Clinton for the nomination, but there was no doubt he would be the Democratic candidate. Clinton, in turn, was keeping his valuable vice president. Gore arrived at the convention five days ahead of Clinton. In meetings with various constituents, he demonstrated much-improved public-speaking skills. The man formerly thought of as stiff and dull charmed the crowds with his charisma and enthusiasm. Gore even made fun of himself. During one speech, he demonstrated what he called "The Al Gore version of the Macarena." While the fast-paced Latin dance song played, Gore simply stood still.

During his speeches, Gore subtly compared the relative youth of the Democratic ticket to the aging Dole. "Bill Clinton and I offer ourselves as a bridge to the future," he said. Gore also said that Clinton was "a president with the vision to tackle the real problems that really matter to our families."[5]

After the convention, Gore campaigned in several cities. During a joint appearance with Clinton in

Cleveland, Ohio, Gore delivered an animated, rapid-fire speech. As the crowd cheered and clapped, Clinton laughed so hard that tears came to his eyes. "I do not know what the vice president ate for breakfast this morning," Clinton said when it was his turn to address the crowd. "But if he had two more bites of it, he would have blown the roof off."[6]

After the speech, reporters asked Gore what had led to his energized performance. "I have benefited from low expectations," the vice president joked. "Don't blow it for me."[7] Then he added, "I've grown as a public servant and a communicator. . . . These campaigns force those who want the confidence of the American people to go out and really work hard and hustle and make a connection with the American people and respond to them. If you throw your whole heart into that, you can't help but learn a lot in the process."[8] Gore's vibrance continued when he debated Kemp in the fall. His performance was called "superbly vice presidential."[9]

On the first Tuesday in November 1996, American voters went to the polls. Dole earned 41 percent of the vote, but that was not enough. Bill Clinton and Al Gore were reelected as president and vice president. In his acceptance speech, Clinton called Gore "the finest vice president this country has ever seen."[10]

The Democrats' first term in office had been difficult. Unfortunately, harder times were on the horizon. Fund-raising during the reelection campaign came under attack. Gore, in particular, was criticized for making phone calls from the White House. It is illegal for federal employees to solicit money in federal buildings. In March 1997, Gore appeared on national television and admitted his mistakes. However, he appeared stiff and unapologetic. He used the term "no controlling legal authority" several times. It was his attempt to explain how he misunderstood the complicated rules governing campaign contributions.

The fund-raiser at the Buddhist temple in April 1996 also raised concerns. It was illegal because the temple was a tax-exempt building. Gore said it was an honest mistake that he attended the fund-raiser. He thought it was simply a community event. The Democratic National Committee eventually returned the money that was raised during that event.

FBI director Louis Freeh was among those who said Attorney General Janet Reno should appoint a special prosecutor to investigate the fund-raising episodes. The media dubbed the controversy "Donorgate." "There's a clear-cut case for a prosecution of Gore," said Charles Lewis of the Center for Public Integrity. "In Washington, they call it spin. In other places, we call that lying."[11]

Some people defended Gore. They said that Gore's activities were not illegal; the only problem was where he had conducted them. If he had not used a government office to make the fund-raising calls, he would not be in trouble.[12]

In June 1997, a group of environmentalists charged that Gore had not pushed hard enough for tougher air-pollution standards or more stringent control of "greenhouse gases." The gases, carbon dioxide and methane, keep heat trapped in the earth. They are believed to be responsible for global warming.

The environmentalists warned Gore through the press that they would not support him in the year 2000 unless he took more action. "What we need and what we expect is leadership," said Deb Callahan of the League of Conservation Voters. "Not to speak out and not to influence the President is not leadership. It is a bit perplexing that [Gore] would step back from providing this leadership."[13] The environmentalists "should have a little faith," responded Gore's chief of staff. "[Gore's] views on the environment have never been about votes or having things in his pocket, but about an agenda he deeply and personally believes in."[14]

Gore met with some environmentalists at the White House. When one said that it would be good for Gore's political future if he listened to them, Gore cut the speaker off. "Don't go down that road," Gore replied. "I am committed to this cause, and I am not going to decide what we should do based on whether it will get me elected."[15]

In July 1997, Al and Tipper Gore gathered with friends and family at National Cathedral in Washington, D.C. There, the Gores' eldest daughter, Karenna, married Andrew Schiff, a doctor from New York City. It was a day of celebration, but controversy soon arose again.

In October 1997, Gore met with leaders of the entertainment industry. During the meeting, the vice president spoke about the television show *Ellen*. The show's star, Ellen DeGeneres, had recently revealed that she was a lesbian. Her character on the show also "came out of the closet." Gore said that because of the program, "millions of Americans were forced to look at sexual orientation in a more open light."[16] His comments angered and offended many, who thought he was supporting homosexuality.

In early December 1997, Attorney General Reno announced that she would not appoint a special prosecutor for "Donorgate." She said that President Clinton's calls did not violate Justice Department guidelines, and Vice President Gore's calls were to solicit what is called soft money. Soft money is not subject to federal rules. Reno said some of the soft money was put into campaign accounts, which are regulated. However, Gore did not know that was going to be done, Reno said. "The president and the White House believe they are doing the appropriate thing to

Attorney General Janet Reno, right, dismissed claims that Clinton and Gore had acted illegally while raising campaign money.

correct any mistakes they've identified," Clinton's spokesman said.[17]

Gore was vindicated, but not for long. In August 1998, Justice Department investigators obtained notes that seemed to contradict Gore's accounts of his fund-raising phone calls. Reno decided to study again whether an independent prosecutor needed to be named. "Al Gore has always been Mr. Clean," said one Democratic consultant. "He's in danger [politically] unless he breaks out of this."[18] Clinton, too, was worried about Gore. "The President loves the guy and will do anything to help him," said one Clinton aide. "He also wants him to be elected in 2000."[19]

Clinton would not fret over Gore for long. Soon, the president would be consumed by his own woes. In April 1998, a federal judge dismissed Paula Jones's lawsuit against the president. The judge said that if Jones's charges were true, then Clinton's actions had been rude and crude. They were not illegal, though, the judge declared.

Clinton had already testified in a deposition for the lawsuit. He had been asked about his sex life. Jones's lawyers wanted to prove that Clinton had a pattern of sexual misbehavior. They heard rumors that Clinton once had a sexual relationship with a young White House intern named Monica Lewinsky. In sworn testimony, Clinton denied he had a relationship with Ms. Lewinsky. He also denied that he asked her to lie about their situation. Clinton further denied that he had helped Ms. Lewinsky find a job to buy her silence. That testimony would turn Clinton's presidency upside down.

10

Looking Ahead

$\mathbf{U}$ntil the late summer of 1998, Al Gore's future seemed almost assured. He would finish out his term as vice president of the United States. Then, he would win the Democratic nomination for president in the year 2000. Gore's intelligence, high moral standards, and vast experience would make him a tough candidate to beat.

"He is in an incredibly strong position," a member of the Democratic National Committee said in 1996. "A sitting vice president always has the advantage of political infrastructure, visibility and four years to make the administration agenda his own, using the bully pulpit more than anyone else except the president."[1]

That was before "Donorgate" and the Monica Lewinsky scandal. As Gore neared the end of his sixth year in office, his political life was in upheaval. Attorney General Janet Reno had considered whether to name a special prosecutor to look into Clinton's and Gore's fund-raising activities during the 1996 campaign. Although Reno had found no need to investigate the matter further, new evidence had then caused her to reopen the case. Gore received good news in November 1998, when Reno concluded again that there was no need for more investigation. Reno said there was clear and convincing evidence that Gore had not lied about his actions. "The vice president is pleased," said Gore spokesman Christopher Lehane.[2] Yet the scandal still could cause damage to Gore's image as the 2000 election neared.

Gore also faced problems from the Lewinsky scandal. Because his career was linked to Clinton's, any bad news for the president could also cause Gore grief. Lewinsky, a former White House intern, and President Clinton both denied under oath that they had a sexual affair. Their legal statements were taken as part of Paula Jones's sexual harassment lawsuit against Clinton.

Clinton continued to deny a relationship with Lewinsky. During a televised press conference, he adamantly stated that he never had sexual relations with her. He also called his Cabinet members and other top Democrats to a special White House meeting. There, he assured them the charges were false.

"He is the president of the country," Gore said. "He is also my friend. And I want to ask you now, every single one of you, to join me in supporting him and standing by his side."[3]

By the summer of 1998, reports surfaced that

Lewinsky was going to change her testimony and admit to having had an affair with the president. Several weeks later, Clinton admitted it as well. He went on national television to say he lied. He also asked for forgiveness. Still, his betrayal was stunning. "I was present in the Roosevelt Room . . . when the president categorically denied any sexual involvement with Monica Lewinsky," said Democratic senator Dianne Feinstein of California. "I believed him. His remarks . . . leave me with a deep sense of sadness in that my trust in his credibility has been badly shattered."[4]

A few days after Clinton's admission, special

The Gore family at home, from right: Kristin, Sarah, Tipper, Al, Albert III, and Karenna with her husband, Andrew Schiff.

prosecutor Kenneth Starr sent to Congress his report on the Lewinsky matter. It was published in newspapers and over the Internet. The report contained graphic and shocking details about the Clinton-Lewinsky relationship. Starr said the details were necessary to show the extent to which Clinton had lied.

Starr's report concluded there was overwhelming evidence that President Clinton tried to obstruct the judicial process and that his actions were criminal. The report cited the president's actions in the Jones lawsuit as well as the grand jury investigation. Lawmakers began talking about impeachment. To impeach is to accuse a high official of a crime.

The first step in the impeachment process is for the House Judiciary Committee to investigate the matter. If the committee votes to proceed, members of the House of Representatives then consider the motion. If the motion passes in the House, the Senate then votes. A two-thirds vote in the Senate is needed to convict. Upon conviction, the official is removed from office.

In early December 1998, the House Judiciary Committee voted to proceed with impeachment. If Clinton were convicted, Gore would become president. Yet his association with a fallen president could lead voters to support other candidates in the 2000 election.

Public opinion polls taken a few days after the Starr report was released showed that a majority of Americans did not want to see President Clinton impeached. However, they believed some sort of punishment was appropriate. Gore also spoke out against impeachment. "I do not believe this [Starr] report serves as the basis for overturning the judgment of the American people . . . that Bill Clinton should be their president," he said.[5]

It was ironic that Gore's political future rested on Clinton's character. Gore himself always had an immaculate reputation. In the media, he was frequently called "squeaky clean" and a Boy Scout. His biggest problem seemed to be improving his public-speaking skills. Gore's mother, Pauline, once said that if Clinton were ever to be irreparably damaged, "[Al] will be damaged politically. But the important things about Al will not be damaged. His character, his ability, his honesty, his integrity."[6]

Gore faced a personal loss in December 1998. His father, Al Gore, Sr., died of natural causes at the age of ninety. Tipper and Al Jr. were at his bedside.

On February 12, 1999, President Clinton was found not guilty by the Senate on both counts of impeachment: perjury and obstruction of justice. With great public support, he triumphed over one of the greatest presidential scandals in history. Did his vice president emerge unscathed? Clinton himself was eager to separate Gore from the wrongdoings. "Any mistakes . . . were my fault," he said shortly after his acquittal.[7]

Yet there is perhaps an even bigger obstacle Gore faces in his quest for the presidency. He is up against history. In 1836, Martin Van Buren became the first sitting vice president to be elected president. It did not happen again until 1988, when Vice President George Bush was elected president. With those odds,

Gore is a long shot to become the first president of the new millennium.

Those who knew him well believed that if anyone could beat the odds, it would be Al Gore. As he faced the biggest challenge of his political career, there was little doubt that Gore would do what Gore did best: focus on the problem and find the best possible solution. "I've always been committed to excellence," Gore once said. "I believed in the old saying 'The harder I work, the luckier I get.'"[8]

Al Gore has his eye on the White House for the new millennium.

Chronology

1948— Albert Arnold Gore, Jr., is born on March 31 in Washington, D.C.

1965— Graduates from St. Albans School for Boys in Washington, D.C.; meets Mary Elizabeth "Tipper" Aitcheson; enters Harvard University in Cambridge, Massachusetts.

1969— Graduates from Harvard, enlists in the United States Army, and reports for duty at Fort Rucker in Alabama.

1970— Al and Tipper are married on May 19.

1971— Serves six months in Vietnam; resigns from the military after returning home in June; moves to Nashville and begins working as a reporter for the *Tennessean*; also begins divinity courses at Vanderbilt University.

1973— First child, Karenna, is born in August; leaves divinity school and enters Vanderbilt Law School.

1976— Announces his candidacy for the United States House of Representatives, wins the race, and moves with Tipper and Karenna to Washington, D.C.

1977— Second child, Kristin, is born in June.

1978— Runs unopposed for a second term in office.

1979— Daughter Sarah is born in January.

1980— Elected to his third term in Congress.

1982— Son, Albert III, is born in October; reelected to a fourth term.

1984— Gore wins election to the United States Senate; Tipper Gore forms the Parents' Music Resource Center.

1987— Announces his candidacy for president of the United States.

1988— Withdraws his bid for the presidential nomination after the New York primary.

1989— Albert Gore, III, is hit by a car and severely injured.

1990— Reelected to the Senate.

1992— *Earth in the Balance* is published and becomes a best-seller; chosen to be Bill Clinton's running mate; elected vice president of the United States.

1993 — Gore and Clinton are sworn into office; Gore prepares a plan to "reinvent" government; debates the North American Free Trade Agreement with Ross Perot on *Larry King Live*.

1994 — Ongoing efforts to promote family and medical leave; negotiates with television executives to establish a voluntary ratings system for their programs and to increase children's programming on television.

1995 — Continues to lead administration's efforts to connect the nation's libraries and classrooms to the Internet, to clean up and protect the environment, to reduce nuclear arsenals around the world.

1996 — Clinton and Gore are reelected to office; Congress passes the historic Telecommunications Act; Gore chairs the White House Commission on Aviation Safety and Security; continues efforts on Community Empowerment—special tax breaks and incentives to attract businesses to urban and rural areas.

1997— Works to enact tough measures to prevent tobacco sales to children; calls for an Electronic Bill of Rights to protect personal privacy online.

1998 — Supports Children's On Line Privacy Protection Act to prohibit commercial Web sites from gathering personal information from children without parental permission; father, Albert Gore, Sr., dies in December.

1999 — Declares his candidacy for the Democratic nomination for president.

Chapter Notes

Chapter 1. A Fateful Phone Call

1. Sandra McElwaine, "Her Life, Her Love Story," *Good Housekeeping*, March 1993, p. 236.

2. Ibid.

3. Walter Shapiro, "Gore: A Hard-Won Sense of Ease," *Time*, July 20, 1992, p. 28.

Chapter 2. Big Al, Little Al

1. Sidney Shallett, "He Licked the Old Man of the Senate," *Saturday Evening Post*, October 1, 1957, p. 67.

2. Ibid.

3. Al Gore, "Facing the Crisis of Spirit," *Vital Speeches of the Day*, August 15, 1992, p. 647.

4. Alex S. Jones, "Al Gore's Double Life," *The New York Times Magazine*, October 25, 1992, p. 44.

5. Bill Hewitt, "Tennessee Waltz," *People*, November 16, 1992, p. 99.

6. Sherrye Henry, "Talking to . . . Albert Gore Jr.," *Vogue*, May 1988, p. 56.

7. Jennet Conant, "Family First," *Redbook*, March 1994, p. 82.

8. Ibid.

9. Ibid.

10. Sandra McElwaine, "Her Life, Her Love Story," *Good Housekeeping*, March 1993, p. 235.

11. "From Arms Control to Twisted Sister," *U.S. News and World Report*, February 15, 1988, p. 17.

12. Henry, p. 56.

13. Strobe Talbott, "Trying to Set Himself Apart," *Time*, October 19, 1987, p. 17.

14. Gore, p. 647.

Chapter 3. Reporting for Duty

1. David Holwerk, "How the Country Works," *The Nation*, February 2, 1974, p. 135.

2. Hank Hillin, *Al Gore Jr.: Born to Lead* (Nashville, Tenn.: Pine Hall Press, 1988), p. 78.

3. David Maraniss, "As a Reporter, Gore Found a Reason to Be in Politics," *The Washington Post*, January 4, 1998, p. A-1.

4. Alex S. Jones, "Al Gore's Double Life," *The New York Times Magazine*, October 25, 1992, p. 79.

5. Hillin, p. 79.

6. Maraniss, p. A-1.

7. Sherrye Henry, "Talking to . . . Albert Gore Jr.," *Vogue*, May 1988, p. 62.

8. Jones, p. 79.

9. Ibid.

10. Peter J. Boyer, "The Political Scene: Gore's Dilemma," *The New Yorker*, November 28, 1994, p. 103.

11. Ibid.

12. Hillin, p. 101.

13. Strobe Talbott, "Trying to Set Himself Apart," *Time*, October 19, 1987, p. 18.

Chapter 4. On the Political Scene

1. Sandra McElwaine, "Her Life, Her Love Story," *Good Housekeeping*, March 1993, p. 235.

2. Sherrye Henry, "Talking to . . . Albert Gore Jr.," *Vogue*, May 1988, p. 56.

3. Eric Pooley and Karen Tumulty, "Can Al Bare His Soul?" *Time*, December 15, 1997, pp. 44–45.

4. Kenneth T. Walsh, "Seven New Senators Take Their Stands," *U.S. News and World Report*, April 15, 1985, p. 37.

5. Timothy Noah, "A Washington Tale: Gore Chic," *Newsweek*, February 16, 1987, p. 20.

6. Strobe Talbott, "Trying to Set Himself Apart," *Time*, October 19, 1987, p. 18.

7. Tom Humphrey, "Gore Becoming More at Ease, 'Just Being Himself,' Wife Says," *Knoxville (Tennessee) News Sentinel*, August 30, 1996 (article obtained from NewsBank NewsFile).

8. Marci McDonald, "A Fighting Democrat," *Maclean's*, October 26, 1987, p. 32.

9. McElwaine, p. 234.

10. "From Arms Control to Twisted Sister," *U.S. News and World Report*, February 15, 1988, p. 17.

11. Noah, p. 20.

12. "Whistling Dixie," *Time*, April 6, 1987, p. 32.

13. "An Early Lock on Veep, At Least," *Time*, January 18, 1988, p. 20.

14. Richard L. Berke, "The Good Son," *The New York Times Magazine*, February 20, 1994, p. 44.

15. Al Gore, *Earth in the Balance: Ecology and the Human Spirit* (New York: Penguin Books, 1992), p. 8.

16. Morton M. Kondracke, "Southern Strategist," *New Republic*, December 7, 1987, p. 21.

Chapter 5. Failure and Heartache

1. Bill Turque, "The Three Faces of Al Gore," *Newsweek*, July 20, 1992, p. 30.

2. "Nice Young Man," *New Republic*, June 1, 1987, p. 4.

3. Henry Hertzberg, "Tipper De Doo Dah," *New Republic*, December 7, 1987, pp. 22–23.

4. Jack W. Germond and Jules Witcover, *Whose Broad Stripes and Bright Stars? The Trivial Pursuit of the Presidency, 1988* (New York: Warner Books, 1989), p. 225.

5. Marci McDonald, "A Fighting Democrat," *Maclean's*, October 26, 1987, p. 31.

6. Michael Kramer, "Is America Ready for a Boy President?" *U.S. News and World Report*, February 29, 1988, p. 15.

7. Morton M. Kondracke, "Southern Strategist," *New Republic*, December 7, 1987, p. 20.

8. Kramer, p. 15.

9. Hugh Sidey, "Sons of the Fathers," *Time*, March 7, 1988, p. 22.

10. Turque, p. 31.

11. "The Mayor's Runaway Mouth," *Newsweek*, May 2, 1988, p. 25.

12. Germond and Witcover, p. 314.

13. Jonathan Alter with Eleanor Clift, "Goodbye—for Now—to Gore," *Newsweek*, May 2, 1988, p. 25.

14. Bill Hewitt, "Tennessee Waltz," *People*, November 16, 1992, p. 102.

15. Walter Shapiro, "Gore: A Hard-Won Sense of Ease," *Time*, July 20, 1992, p. 28.

16. Richard Lacayo, "The Other Partner: Tipper," *Time*, July 20, 1992, p. 20.

17. Al Gore, *Earth in the Balance: Ecology and the Human Spirit* (New York: Penguin Books, 1992), pp. 8–9.

18. Ibid., p. 16.

19. Al Gore, "Facing the Crisis of Spirit," *Vital Speeches of the Day*, August 15, 1992, p. 648.

20. Gail McKnight, "Tipper Gore: The Vice President's First Lady," *The Saturday Evening Post*, March/April 1993, p. 77.

21. Shapiro, p. 28.

22. Ibid.

Chapter 6. Back in the Race

1. Michael Kramer, "Is America Ready for a Boy President?" *U.S. News and World Report*, February 29, 1988, p. 15.

2. Alex S. Jones, "Al Gore's Double Life," *The New York Times Magazine*, October 25, 1992, p. 43.

3. Eleanor Clift, "Desperately Seeking Southerners," *Newsweek*, May 13, 1991, p. 33.

4. Jones, p. 43.

5. Ibid.

6. Ibid.

7. Ibid.

8. Elizabeth Gleick and Margie Sellinger, "Tipper's Return," *People*, July 27, 1992, p. 34.

9. Jennet Conant, "Family First," *Redbook*, March 1994, p. 132.

10. Sandra McElwaine, "Her Life, Her Love Story," *Good Housekeeping*, March 1993, p. 236.

11. Bob Woodward, *The Agenda: Inside the Clinton White House* (New York: Simon & Schuster, 1994), p. 53.

12. *Bartlett's Familiar Quotations*, 16th ed. (Boston: Little, Brown and Company, 1992), p. 338.

13. Bill Turque, "How to Stay in the Loop," *Newsweek*, October 26, 1992, p. 27.

14. Woodward, p. 53.

15. Ibid.

16. Meg Greenfield, "The Democratic Fortysomethings," *Newsweek*, July 20, 1992, p. 70.

17. Al Gore, "Facing the Crisis of Spirit," *Vital Speeches of the Day*, August 15, 1992, p. 648.

18. Richard L. Berke, "The Good Son," *The New York Times Magazine*, February 20, 1994, p. 35.

19. Joe Klein, "Running Mates," *Newsweek*, July 20, 1992, p. 23.

Chapter 7. "Excellent Adventure"

1. Jennet Conant, "Family First," *Redbook*, March 1994, p. 82.

2. Bob Woodward, *The Agenda: Inside the Clinton White House* (New York: Simon & Schuster, 1994), p. 54.

3. Jack W. Germond and Jules Witcover, *Mad as Hell: Revolt at the Ballot Box 1992* (New York: Warner Books, 1993), p. 383.

4. Eleanor Clift, "Playing Second Fiddle," *Newsweek*, January 25, 1993, p. 35.

5. S. C. Gwynne and Elizabeth Taylor, "We're Not Measuring the Drapes," *Time*, October 19, 1992, p. 36.

6. Al Gore, *Earth in the Balance: Ecology and the Human Spirit* (New York: Penguin Books, 1992), pp. iii.

7. Ibid., p. xvi.

8. Gwynne and Taylor, p. 36.

9. Stanley W. Cloud, "Quayle vs. Gore," *Time*, October 19, 1992, p. 35.

10. Ibid., p. 34.

11. Dan Goodgame, "Quayle vs. Gore," *Time*, August 3, 1992, p. 38.

12. Bill Turque, "How to Stay in the Loop," *Newsweek*, October 26, 1992, p. 27.

13. Gwynne and Taylor, p. 36.

14. Elizabeth Gleick and Margie Sellinger, "Tipper's Return," *People*, July 27, 1992, p. 34.

15. Ibid.

Chapter 8. The First Four Years

1. Richard L. Berke, "The Good Son," *The New York Times Magazine*, February 20, 1994, p. 30.

2. Eleanor Clift, "Playing Second Fiddle," *Newsweek*, January 25, 1993, p. 35.

3. Walter Shapiro, "Has Anyone Seen This Man?" *Esquire*, September 1993, p. 117.

4. Matthew Cooper and Paul Glastris, "Al Gore's Biggest Fix," *U.S. News and World Report*, September 13, 1993, pp. 40–41.

5. Berke, p. 57.

6. Ibid.

7. Michael Duffy, "Al's Secret Debating Tricks," *Time*, November 22, 1993, p. 41.

8. Berke, p. 35.

9. Duffy, p. 41.

10. Eleanor Clift, "The Reinvention of Al Gore," *Newsweek*, September 13, 1993, p. 39.

11. Ibid.

12. Shapiro, p. 116.

13. Bob Woodward, *The Agenda: Inside the Clinton White House* (New York: Simon & Schuster, 1994), p. 280.

14. Berke, p. 33.

15. J. F. O. McAllister, "A Veep Who Leaves Prints," *Time*, September 2, 1996, p. 37.

16. Shapiro, p. 117.

17. Woodward, p. 327.

18. Ibid., p. 148.

19. Bob Woodward, *The Choice* (New York: Simon & Schuster, 1996), p. 16.

Chapter 9. Four More Years

1. Bob Woodward, *The Choice* (New York: Simon & Schuster, 1996), p. 49.

2. Ibid., p. 347.

3. Ibid., p. 262.

4. Ibid.

5. Thomas Hardy, "Is 4 More Enough for Gore?" *Chicago Tribune*, August 29, 1996, p. 13.

6. Elizabeth Shogren, "Campaign '96: A Liberating Experience for Gore," *Los Angeles Times*, November 7, 1996, p. A-16.

7. Ibid.

8. Ibid.

9. Joe Klein, "Second Bananahood," *Newsweek*, October 21, 1996, p. 42.

10. Shogren, p. A-16.

11. Richard S. Dunham, "Al Gore: The Boy Scout Who Wasn't Prepared for Donorgate," *Business Week*, September 15, 1997, p. 54.

12. Mortimer B. Zuckerman, "The Vice President as Fall Guy," *U.S. News and World Report*, October 6, 1997, p. 84.

13. "Environmental Groups Say Gore Has Not Measured Up to the Job," *The New York Times*, June 22, 1997, p. 16.

14. Ibid.

15. Howard Fineman and Karen Breslau, "Gore Feels the Heat," *Newsweek*, October 27, 1997, p. 25.

16. Ibid., p. 26.

17. Lance Gay, "Democrats Give Back $1.5 Million in Campaign Funds," *Scripps Howard News Service*, February 28, 1997 (article obtained from NewsBank NewsFile).

18. Dunham, p. 54.

19. Jeffrey H. Birnbaum, "The President Loves the Guy," *Fortune*, October 27, 1997, p. 62.

Chapter 10. Looking Ahead

1. Thomas Hardy, "Is 4 More Enough for Gore?" *Chicago Tribune*, August 29, 1996, p. 13.

2. Michael J. Sniffen, "Reno Rejects Investigation of Gore," *Associated Press*, <http://www.ap.org> (November 24, 1998).

3. Richard L. Berke, "The Gore Guide to the Future," *The New York Times Magazine*, February 22, 1998, p. 32.

4. *The New York Times* News Service, "Prominent Democrats Unhappy with Clinton," *The Richmond Times-Dispatch*, August 19, 1998, p. A-9.

5. Associated Press, "Clinton Counterattacks," *The Richmond Times-Dispatch*, September 13, 1998, p. A-8.

6. Peter J. Boyer, "Gore's Dilemma," *The New Yorker*, November 28, 1994, p. 110.

7. Richard L. Berke, "Lewinsky Ordeal May Have Put Gore on Firmer Ground for 2000," *The New York Times*, February 17, 1999, p. A-12.

8. Sherrye Henry, "Talking to . . . Albert Gore Jr.," *Vogue*, May 1988, p. 56.

Further Reading

Berke, Richard L. "The Gore Guide to the Future." *The New York Times Magazine*, February 2, 1998, pp. 33–70.

Germond, Jack W., and Jules Witcover. *Mad as Hell: Revolt at the Ballot Box, 1992*. New York: Warner Books, 1993.

———. *Whose Broad Stripes and Bright Stars? The Trivial Pursuit of the Presidency 1988*. New York: Warner Books, 1989.

Gore, Al. *Earth in the Balance: Ecology and the Human Spirit*. New York: Penguin Books, 1992.

Hillin, Hank. *Al Gore: Born to Lead*. Nashville, Tenn.: Pine Hall Press, 1988.

Jones, Alex S. "Al Gore's Double Life." *The New York Times Magazine*, October 25, 1992, pp. 40–79.

Kelly, Michael, and Maureen Dowd. "The Company He Keeps." *The New York Times Magazine*, January 17, 1993, pp. 22–26.

Klein, Joe. "Running Mates." *Newsweek*, July 20, 1992, pp. 20-25.

Kramer, Barbara. *Tipper Gore: Activist, Author, Photographer*. Springfield, N.J.: Enslow Publishers, Inc., 1999.

Pooley, Eric, and Karen Tumulty. "Can Al Bare His Soul?" *Time*, December 15, 1997, pp. 44–51.

Woodward, Bob. *The Agenda: Inside the Clinton White House*. New York: Simon & Schuster, 1994.

———. *The Choice*. New York: Simon & Schuster, 1996.

Internet Addresses

"Welcome to the White House: An Interactive Citizens' Handbook"

<http://www.whitehouse.gov/WH/html/handbook.html>

Vice President Gore's Home Page

<http://www.whitehouse.gov/WH/EOP/OVP/index.html>

To send e-mail to the vice president

<vice.president@whitehouse.gov>

To send mail to the vice president

The White House Office of the Vice President
Old Executive Office Building
Washington, D.C. 20501.

Index